Getting Ready for Sunday:
A Practical Guide for Worship Planning

GETTING READY FOR SUNDAY:
A *PRACTICAL* *GUIDE* *for* *WORSHIP* *PLANNING*

MARTIN THIELEN

BROADMAN PRESS
Nashville, Tennessee

© Copyright 1989 • Broadman Press

All rights reserved

4223-19

ISBN: 0-8054-2319-2

Dewey Decimal Classification: 251.01

Subject heading: SERMONS // PREACHING

Library of Congress Catalog Card Number: 88-19808

Printed in the United States of America

Library of Congress Cataloging-in-Publication Data

Thielen, Martin, 1956-

    Getting ready for Sunday : a practical guide for worship planning

/ Martin Thielen.

    p. cm.

    ISBN 0-8054-2319-2

    1. Public worship. 2. Worship programs. I. Title.

BV15.T45 1989

264—dc19   88-19808

Dedication

To Paula, partner in life
To Dill, partner in worship leadership

Preface

At a denominational convention, two old seminary friends ran into each other. It had been twenty years since they last met. One was now a pastor, the other a minister of music. The pastor asked the music minister, "What have you been doing these past twenty years?" He answered, "The same as you, getting ready for Sunday!"

The sole purpose of this book is to help worship leaders get ready for Sunday. It is unapologetically pragmatic. This book is not on the theology of worship but on the practice of worship. While good books are available on the subject of worship, few have a practical slant. This book was written to help fill that void. It comes out of my experience as a pastor and worship leader. It was written for pastors, ministers of music, and others who plan and lead worship. If it can help you prepare and lead more meaningful worship services, then its purpose will have been accomplished.

Contents

Introduction

As prime minister of England, Winston Churchill sat through many sessions of Parliament. A story is told about one particular session. A member of Parliament was giving an extremely long and boring speech. He noticed that Churchill had laid his head down on the table. Assuming that Churchill was asleep, the man became quite angry.

He said to the Parliament, "Here we are, discussing one of the great issues of our country; and our prime minister is sleeping."

After a long pause, Churchill, never raising his head, said, "I wish to God I were."

Unfortunately, many people have similiar feelings when they attend worship services. Worship has become boring and stagnant in many churches. A growing number of worship leaders are concerned about this. I recently helped lead a worship seminar in my state. The worship leaders who attended had a deep desire to enhance the quality of their worship services. What they most wanted were practical ideas for improving worship. While there are many excellent resources on worship, they usually focus on theory, history, and theology. We need historical and theological foundations, but we also need practical and concrete help. That's the purpose of this book. It was written to provide a pragmatic approach for getting ready for Sunday.

The underlying presupposition behind this book is that worship is the greatest priority of the church. Everything else flows from it. The church has a great mission. That mission begins, however, with the worship of God.

Consider the example of Noah. When Noah finally came off the ark, he had a whole new world to explore and develop. There was much to be done. Noah's first priority, however, was to worship God (Gen 8:18-22). The same should be true for us. The church has much work to do in the kingdom of God. It begins with worship.

Nothing is more important in the life of the church than the worship of God.

Worship is a priority for the church. Worship also has great potential. When we worship, we encounter the living Lord. Such an encounter has tremendous possibilities. Worship affirms the reality and greatness of God, celebrates the work of Christ, and allows the Spirit to touch our lives. Worship can renew, encourage, inspire, challenge, comfort, and heal. It can redirect our lives, clarify our values and loyalties, and add meaning to our existence. Corporate worship reminds us that we are not alone but part of a community of faith, members of the family of God. These good gifts and more are possible in the worship event. Getting ready for Sunday's worship service demands our best efforts as worship leaders. It is our highest priority. Its potential is hard to exaggerate.

With these preliminary remarks behind, let me briefly introduce you to the format of this book. Chapter 1 deals with constructing a worship outline. An outline gives flow and movement to a worship service. It is foundational in getting ready for Sunday. The next step is to fill in the outline with various elements of worship. This is the subject of chapter 2. Chapter 3 contains completed orders of worship which were developed using this process. In chapter 4 are examples of how other worship leaders operate. Some of their planning procedures are discussed. Examples of their worship services are also included.

At this point I want to mention a possible concern. Some worship leaders are cautious about changing the order of worship in their church. They are afraid the congregation may not approve. I would like to make several comments concerning this issue.

First, do not assume that changing worship patterns will cause a problem. When I came to my present church, they had followed the same order of worship for twenty years. The only changes made were hymn selections. When I began to change that pattern, the response was positive. People were happy to see us make some meaningful changes. A few people may object to changes in the worship service, but some people object to everything!

Second, remember that your primary calling is to be the worship leader of your congregation. You have a God-given responsibility to lead your church in worship. If you feel that changes are necessary or that they will enhance worship, it is appropriate for you to initiate those changes. Obviously, tactfulness and sensitivity are necessary, but a congregation can be led to change its worship pattern.

Third, let me suggest a practical way to implement change. If you want to change your worship services but are still hesitant, try doing it in small steps. For example, experiment with innovation and variety during the Christmas season. That would be a non-threatening, short-term experiment. Then feel out your congregation. How did they like it? If you find support (and I believe you will), you can then lead your church to make ongoing changes.

Finally, never change worship patterns simply for the sake of change. Innovation and creativity are not to be ends in themselves. The only reason to change worship is to improve and enhance it.

It is my prayer that God will use this book to help you do a better job of getting ready for Sunday. Let the worship begin!

1

Outlining the Worship Service

A funny thing happened in my first pastorate. One Sunday night the deacons decided to purchase sixty tons of gravel for our church's parking lot. The gravel was ordered on Monday and was to arrive by 5:00 PM on Tuesday. Tuesday evening came, but the gravel did not. I called the man from whom we had ordered the gravel and informed him that it had not yet arrived.

"But it's already been delivered," he said.

"Well," I replied, "it's not here."

He sounded worried. "This is the pastor of Grace Baptist Church isn't it?" he asked.

"No," I said, "this is the pastor of First Baptist Church." Grace Baptist Church was pleased to have their parking lot re-covered at no cost!

This story reminds us of an important principle. If we do not know where we are going, we are not likely to get there. Worse yet, we may end up at the wrong place. This is true in the area of worship. We need to know where we are headed and be intentional about getting there. What is the destination of the worship event? The answer for me is simple: to encounter the living Lord. The goal of worship is for God's people to experience His presence as Isaiah did when he "saw the Lord . . . high and lifted up" (Isa. 6:1), or like Thomas when he confessed, "My Lord and my God!" (John 20:28).

A worship outline can help your congregation encounter the living Lord. The worship outline is the road map and guide for the worship event. It helps lead a congregation through the movements of worship. A good worship outline can go a long way toward developing meaningful worship services. It is an important step in getting ready for Sunday.

When I begin preparing for a worship service, I start by constructing a worship outline. After experimenting for several years with various orders of worship, I have been drawn to a particular style of outlining. I block the worship service into several movements by the use of interpretative categories. There is nothing particularly holy about this method, but I have found it to be extremely effective. It helps interpret to your congregation what they are doing. It gives flow and movement to the service. It offers variety. It also looks impressive on paper. The worship outline is a visual aid to help your people worship.

Outlining worship into several movements is consistent with Scripture and church tradition. One of the best examples of worship is described in the sixth chapter of Isaiah. There were several movements in Isaiah's worship experience. It began with the praise of God. Biblical worship must be God centered. It should affirm the glory and majesty of God. Isaiah also had a time of prayer. In this case it was a prayer of confession. The third movement of this worship experience was proclamation. Isaiah heard the voice of the Lord. The last movement was a time of surrender and commitment. True worship calls God's people to service. This model of worship points out at least four distinct movements: praise, prayer, proclamation, and commitment. When we plan worship services today, we should lead our congregation through these and other movements of worship. The worship outline is an excellent tool for accomplishing this.

Soren Kierkegaard once described worship in terms of a drama. He said that in most churches the congregation tends to be an audience. Although this may be the usual approach, it is wrong. Kierkegaard suggested that the proper model is for the congregation to be the actors. This is an important insight. When people worship, they should not be passive spectators. Rather, they should actively participate in the worship of God. If members of the congregation are to be the actors, they need a script. The order of worship is the script for the drama of worship and merits careful attention.

What you will see in this chapter is the basic outline of the service, the "skeleton," so to speak. In the next chapters you will see how to fill in the outline with various elements of worship. A good approach is to develop a worship outline, use it four to six weeks, then change it. After several months or years have passed, you could certainly bring it back and use it again. In this way you can combine familiarity with variety.

It is a good idea to take a few moments at the beginning of the service to interpret the worship outline to your congregation. This can be listed in your order of worship as "Worship theme interpretation."

There are many ways to construct worship outlines. I will discuss four in this chapter. They include: (1) outlines developed from biblical texts, (2) outlines from the hymnal, (3) outlines based on elements of worship, and (4) outlines for special occasions.

OUTLINES DEVELOPED FROM BIBLICAL TEXTS

An excellent method of outlining the worship service is through the use of Scripture. It challenges the imagination and offers endless possibilities. You simply take a text and construct an outline from it. The sermon text would be a possibility. Several examples follow.

Isaiah 6:1-8 is a classical example of worship at its best. Clearly, Isaiah had an encounter with the living Lord. In this passage we see many of the elements of authentic worship. Isaiah was involved in the praise of God. "Holy, holy, holy, is the Lord of hosts" (v. 3). His worship experience led to self-examination: "Woe is me! For I am lost" (v. 5). Isaiah confessed his sin: "I am a man of unclean lips" (v. 5). He also discovered the forgiveness of God: "Your guilt is taken away, and your sin forgiven" (v. 7). Isaiah heard the word of God: "And I heard the voice of the Lord" (v. 8). Isaiah concluded the worship event with an act of surrender and commitment: "Here am I! Send me" (v. 8).

This text serves well as a worship outline. It also helps the congregation better understand the meaning of worship. A possible outline follows. Remember, the following examples are only worship outlines. The completed orders of worship are found in chapter 3.

Isaiah 6:1-8
AN ENCOUNTER WITH THE LIVING LORD

A TIME FOR PRAISE: "I SAW THE LORD, HIGH AND LIFTED UP."

Prelude
Call to worship
Doxology
Invocation
Hymn of praise

A TIME FOR CONFESSION: "WOE IS ME! FOR I AM UNCLEAN."

Discipline of silence
Prayer of confession
Affirmation of forgiveness
Hymn

A TIME FOR HEARING GOD'S WORD: "THEN I HEARD THE VOICE OF THE LORD."

Scripture reading
Anthem
Sermon

A TIME OF COMMITMENT: "HERE AM I! SEND ME."

Invitation
Concerns of the church
Offering
Benediction
Postlude

Although the gospel is intensely personal, it also has social implications. The Old Testament prophets certainly illustrate that. Jesus
was also concerned with social issues. Our worship services should
occasionally focus our attention on these matters. One of the major
social and moral issues of our day is world hunger. Here is a worship
outline based on Matthew 25:31-36, which could be used for World
Hunger Day or a hunger emphasis.

WHEN HE COMES IN HIS GLORY

Prelude
Hymn of praise
Invocation
Concerns of the church

HE WILL SIT ON HIS GLORIOUS THRONE

Chorus
Discipline of silence
The Lord's Prayer
Offertory hymn
Offering

AND HE WILL SAY, "I WAS HUNGRY"

Responsive reading
Children's sermon
Scripture reading
Anthem
Sermon on hunger
Invitation

"AND YOU GAVE ME FOOD"

Distribution of rice bowls for world hunger
Benediction
Postlude

The next outline could be used to help prepare for a revival effort. It could be used several weeks before, during, and after the revival. The text comes from 2 Chronicles 7:14.

In this passage are four conditions necessary for God's people to experience renewal. All four should happen in a good worship experience. The first condition is to humble ourselves. What better way to do this than through praise and adoration of God? When we acknowledge His glory, we realize our smallness and experience humility. The second condition is prayer. Prayer is an important element in worship. The third condition is to seek God's face. As we listen to the Word of God proclaimed in worship and allow ourselves to be sensitive to it, we can truly seek the face of God. The final condition is repentance. Worship should provide an opportunity to repent and make decisions for Christ. This text, then, provides an extremely good outline for worship.

IF MY PEOPLE, WHICH ARE CALLED BY MY NAME

SHALL HUMBLE THEMSELVES,

Prelude
Call to worship
Hymn
Invocation
Concerns of the church
Chorus

AND PRAY,

Hymn
Discipline of silence
Pastoral prayer

AND SEEK MY FACE,

Offertory hymn
Offering
Anthem
Sermon

AND TURN FROM THEIR WICKED WAYS:

Invitation
Benediction
Postlude

THEN WILL I HEAR FROM HEAVEN, AND WILL FORGIVE THEIR SIN AND WILL HEAL THEIR LAND (2 Chron. 7:14, KJV).

A worship outline could be developed around Philippians 4:10-14. Three movements of worship can be emphasized. The praise of God, the giving of gifts, and a word of comfort and encouragement during the time of proclamation.

REJOICE IN THE LORD (Phil. 4:10)

Prelude
Call to worship
Hymn of praise
Welcome and concerns of the church
Praise chorus

IT WAS GOOD OF YOU TO SHARE (Phil. 4:14)

Discipline of silence
Pastoral prayer
Scripture reading on giving
Offertory hymn
Offering

I CAN DO ALL THINGS THROUGH CHRIST WHICH STRENGHTENETH ME (Phil. 4:13, KJV)

Scripture reading
Anthem
Sermon on Philippians 4:13
Invitation hymn
Benediction
Postlude

One Sunday following Easter, I preached from John 20:19-29. This is the passage dealing with Thomas's doubt. Sometimes people can relate more to the pain of Good Friday than to the joy of Easter; some better understand the suffering of the cross than the happiness of the empty tomb. The sermon dealt with the issue of struggling and doubt. Mark 9:14-29 was used as the basis for the worship outline. This is the story where a father brings his son to Jesus for healing. Jesus told him wholeness was possible for his son if he believed. The father cried out, "I believe; help my unbelief!" We can all identify with that. We do believe, but sometimes we struggle with unbelief. The sermon came from the Gospel of John, concerning Thomas's struggle of faith. The worship outline, however, came from the story in Mark's Gospel.

I BELIEVE (Mark 9:24a)

Prelude
Hymn
Baptism service
Hymn
Concerns of the church
Affirmation of faith
Offertory hymn
Offering

HELP MY UNBELIEF! (Mark 9:24b)

Scripture reading
Anthem
Sermon
Invitation
Benediction
Postlude

The Psalms offer great resources for worship outlines. Hundreds of worship outlines could be developed from the Psalms. Consider this one based on Psalm 100.

MAKE A JOYFUL NOISE TO THE LORD (v. 1)
Prelude
Call to worship
Invocation
Hymn
Concerns of the church

ENTER HIS GATES WITH THANKSGIVING (v. 4)
Hymn
Responsive reading
Prayer of thanksgiving
Offertory hymn
Offering

FOR THE LORD IS GOOD (v. 5)
Children's sermon
Scripture reading
Anthem
Sermon

SERVE THE LORD WITH GLADNESS! (v. 2)
Invitation
Benediction
Postlude

Isaiah 40 offers an excellent passage for constructing a worship outline. Consider the following which has a movement of praise, of prayer and silence, and of proclamation. The sermon should be one of encouragement and comfort.

THE LORD, THE CREATOR, FAINTETH NOT (Isa. 40:28, KJV)
Prelude
Call to worship
Hymn of praise
Invocation

THEY THAT WAIT UPON THE LORD (Isa. 40:31a, KJV)
Hymn
Period of silence
Pastoral prayer
Testimony
Scripture reading
Offertory hymn
Offering

SHALL RENEW THEIR STRENGTH (Isa. 40:31b, KJV)
Scripture reading
Solo
Sermon
Hymn of invitation
Benediction
Postlude

A worship service on the theme of confession and repentance could be developed around Psalm 51. If you observe the church calendar, this would be a good outline for the season of Lent. It could, however, be used at any time.

MY MOUTH SHALL SHOW FORTH THY PRAISE (Ps. 51:15)

Prelude
Baptism
Choral call to worship
Invocation
Hymn of praise
Concerns of the church
Hymn

ACCORDING TO THY MERCY BLOT OUT MY TRANSGRESSIONS (Ps. 51:1)

Responsive reading from Psalm 51
Prayer of confession
Affirmation of forgiveness
Hymn

THEN WILT THOU DELIGHT IN RIGHT SACRIFICES (Ps. 51:19)

Scripture reading
Offertory hymn
Offering

CREATE IN ME A CLEAN HEART (Ps. 51:10)

Anthem
Scripture reading
Sermon

A BROKEN AND CONTRITE HEART, O GOD, THOU WILT NOT DESPISE (Ps. 51:17)

Invitation hymn
Benediction
Postlude

I once developed a series of sermons on the Book of Job. The first sermon dealt with Job's faith. We learn from Job that authentic faith is not expecting God to remove all our suffering, but it is trusting God even in difficult circumstances. Faith struggles and asks hard questions but still affirms, "Though he slay me, yet will I trust him" (Job 13:15, KJV).

The second sermon dealt with Job's question. The point of the sermon is that the "why" question is ultimately fruitless. We will never fully understand why bad things happen to good people. A better approach is the "what" question: What can I do now that this has happened? What can I do to cope with the situation?

The third sermon dealt with Job's friends. We can learn from them how to minister to those who suffer. They offer both negative and positive lessons. Job's friends certainly made some mistakes. They would not allow Job to express freely his emotional and spiritual pain. Their theology was inadequate. They wasted energy in trying to explain why Job was hurting. This approach did not help Job at all. But the three friends did some good things. They were concerned when they heard of Job's suffering; they went to be with him; and they listened.

A fourth sermon was preached on Job's pride, and a fifth on Job's struggle with the reality of death and the possibility of eternal life.

After developing the sermons, I sought a worship outline which would hold the sermons together for the duration of the series. At least four movements were needed in the worship outline: (1) a time for praise and adoration of God, (2) a time for prayer and reflection, (3) a time for proclamation of the sermons, and (4) a time for surrender and commitment. After looking through the Book of Job, four passages were found to accomplish these purposes. Here is the worship outline used for this worship series.

JOB WORSHIPED AND SAID, "BLESSED BE THE NAME OF THE LORD" (Job 1:20-21)

Prelude
Call to worship
Hymn of praise
Concerns of the church
Chorus

HEAR THIS, O JOB; STOP AND CONSIDER THE WONDROUS WORKS OF GOD (Job 37:14)

Scripture reading
Silence and meditation
Prayer
Offertory hymn
Offering

THEN THE LORD ANSWERED JOB OUT OF THE WHIRLWIND (Job 38:1)

Dialogue Scripture reading
Anthem
Sermon

THEN JOB REPLIED, "MY EARS HAVE HEARD, MY EYES HAVE SEEN, THEREFORE I REPENT" (Job 42:5-6)

Invitation
Benediction
Postlude

OUTLINES FROM THE HYMNAL

Another excellent resource for constructing worship outlines is to use the hymnal. The Bible and the hymnbook have long been tools of worship in the Christian church. What follows are examples of worship outlines developed from various hymns.

Many motivating factors bring people to worship. The greatest motivation, however, is to worship God simply because He is worthy of our worship. A service emphasizing the greatness of God could be constructed around the hymn "Holy, Holy, Holy."

HOLY, HOLY, HOLY! LORD GOD ALMIGHTY!

Prelude
Call to worship
Doxology
Invocation

EARLY IN THE MORNING OUR SONG SHALL RISE TO THEE;

Solo
Hymn of praise
Offering

HOLY, HOLY, HOLY, MERCIFUL AND MIGHTY!

Scripture reading
Anthem
Sermon on the majesty of God

GOD IN THREE PERSONS, BLESSED TRINITY!

Invitation
Trinitarian affirmation of faith
Benediction
Postlude

An evangelistic service could be developed around the first stanza of the hymn "Just As I Am."

In the first movement of the service, we are reminded of our finitude and sinfulness compared to the greatness and majesty of God. In the second section we hear the good news that God loves us so much that He allowed Christ to die for us. In the third movement an evangelistic appeal is made, inviting persons to respond to the gospel. In the final section an opportunity is given for persons to respond.

JUST AS I AM, WITHOUT ONE PLEA

Prelude
Call to worship
Invocation
Hymn

BUT THAT THY BLOOD WAS SHED FOR ME

Scripture readings on Christ's death
Prayer of confession
Affirmation of forgiveness
Offertory hymn
Offering

AND THAT THOU BIDD'ST ME COME TO THEE

Anthem
Evangelistic sermon or drama

O LAMB OF GOD, I COME! I COME!

Invitation
Benediction
Postlude

People come to worship with many needs. One of the great possibilities of worship is its ability to encourage and strengthen us. The great old hymn "A Mighty Fortress Is Our God" could be used for such a worship service.

A MIGHTY FORTRESS IS OUR GOD

Prelude
Call to worship
Hymn (A Mighty Fortress)
The greeting
Doxology
Invocation
Concerns of the church

A BULWARK NEVER FAILING

Responsive reading on the theme of God's refuge
Chorus
Discipline of silence
Pastoral prayer
Offertory hymn
Offering

OUR HELPER HE, AMID THE FLOOD

Scripture reading
Anthem
Sermon

HIS KINGDOM IS FOREVER

Hymn
Affirmation of faith
Benediction
Postlude

The cross is at the heart of the gospel. When we look at the cross, we see the crucified God who suffers for us and with us. We must remember the passion of our Lord. Holy Week is an especially good time to do this. Consider developing a Palm Sunday, Maundy Thursday, or Good Friday worship outline from the hymn "When I Survey the Wondrous Cross." The observance of the Lord's Supper would be most appropriate during this worship service.

WHEN I SURVEY THE WONDROUS CROSS, ON WHICH THE PRINCE OF GLORY DIED,

Prelude
Call to worship
Invocation
Hymn

SEE FROM HIS HEAD, HIS HANDS, HIS FEET, SORROW AND LOVE FLOW MINGLED DOWN;

Scripture readings from the passion narratives
Solo such as "Were You There?"
The Lord's Supper

LOVE SO AMAZING, SO DIVINE, DEMANDS MY SOUL, MY LIFE, MY ALL

Invitation
Hymn of commitment
Benediction
Postlude

While the primary focus of worship is the greatness of God, worship should also be a time of recommitment and renewal of our vows to God. Consider using the hymn "All to Jesus I Surrender" for a worship outline emphasizing our commitment to Christ.

ALL TO JESUS I SURRENDER

Prelude
Hymn
Invocation
Welcome and concerns
Responsive reading
Hymn

ALL TO HIM I FREELY GIVE

Discipline of silence
Prayer of commitment
Offertory hymn
Offering

MAKE ME SAVIOR WHOLLY THINE

Children's sermon
Scripture reading
Anthem
Sermon

ALL TO THEE, MY BLESSED SAVIOR, I SURRENDER ALL

Invitation hymn
Benediction
Postlude

Here are two more examples of worship outlines based on hymns.
This one comes from "Come, Thou Almighty King."

COME THOU ALMIGHTY KING, HELP US THY NAME TO SING

Prelude
Choral call to worship
Invocation
Hymn of praise
Concerns of the church

HELP US TO PRAISE, FATHER! ALL GLORIOUS, OVER ALL VICTORIOUS

Responsive reading
Solo
Offertory hymn
Offering

COME AND REIGN OVER US, ANCIENT OF DAYS

Anthem
Sermon
Invitation
Benediction
Postlude

Here is another outline based on "Brethren, We Have Met to Worship."

BRETHREN WE HAVE MET TO WORSHIP
Prelude
Call to worship
Invocation
Greetings

AND ADORE THE LORD OUR GOD
Responsive reading
Hymn of praise
Offertory

WILL YOU PRAY WITH ALL YOUR POWER
Chorus
Discipline of silence
Pastoral prayer

WHILE WE TRY TO PREACH THE WORD
Scripture readings
Anthem
Sermon
Invitation
Doxology
Benediction
Postlude

Endless possibilities exist for constructing worship outlines from hymns. Try using some of these for developing your own worship service outlines:

"I Have Decided to Follow Jesus"
"Savior, Like a Shepherd Lead Us"
"Rise Up, O Men of God"
"I Am Thine, O Lord"
"Take My Life, Lead Me, Lord"
"Open My Eyes that I May See"
"Amazing Grace! How Sweet the Sound"
"How Great Thou Art"
"Onward, Christian Soldiers"
"More About Jesus"
"The Savior Is Waiting"

OUTLINES BASED ON ELEMENTS OF WORSHIP

Outlines based on elements of worship lead the congregation through the various elements of worship. One of the benefits of this kind of worship outline is education. It interprets the worship event. It helps teach the congregation what worship is and how to experience it better. Several examples of worship service outlines based on elements of worship follow.

CALL TO WORSHIP

Prelude
Responsive reading
Doxology
Invocation

WORSHIP THROUGH SONG

Solo
Hymn

WORSHIP THROUGH PRAYER

Discipline of silence
Pastoral prayer
The Lord's Prayer

WORSHIP THROUGH GIVING

Offertory hymn
Offering

WORSHIP THROUGH PROCLAMATION

Scripture readings
Anthem
Sermon

WORSHIP THROUGH SURRENDER

Invitation
Benediction
Postlude

ENCOUNTERING THE LIVING LORD THROUGH

PRAISE

Prelude
Call to worship
Invocation
Hymns of praise

THANKSGIVING

Responsive reading
Testimony
Chorus

CONFESSION

Prayer of confession
Affirmation of forgiveness

INTERCESSION AND PETITION

Hymn
Discipline of silence
Pastoral prayer

SURRENDER

Offering
Anthem
Sermon
Invitation
Benediction
Postlude

WE GATHER TO WORSHIP

Prelude
Choral call to worship
Responsive reading
Hymn of praise
Invocation
Testimony

WE OFFER OUR GIFTS

Offertory hymn
Offering

WE LISTEN TO HIS WORD

Scripture readings
Discipline of silence
Anthem
Sermon

WE RESPOND TO HIS CALL

Hymn of invitation
Affirmation of faith

WE DEPART TO SERVE

Benediction
Postlude

THE MINISTRY OF PRAISE
Prelude
Doxology
Invocation
Responsive reading
Hymn of praise
Concerns of the church

THE MINISTRY OF PRAYER
Discipline of silence
Guided pastoral prayer
Hymn

THE MINISTRY OF THE WORD
Old Testament lesson
New Testament lesson

THE MINISTRY OF GIVING
Offertory hymn
Offertory prayer
Offering

THE MINISTRY OF PROCLAMATION
Anthem
Sermon
Invitation
Benediction
Postlude

WE ENTER TO WORSHIP GOD

Prelude
Doxology
Invocation
Concerns of the church
Hymn
Anthem
Prayer
Offertory hymn
Offering

WE LISTEN TO THE WORD OF GOD

Children's sermon
Scripture reading
Sermon
Solo

WE RESPOND TO THE CALL OF GOD

Invitation
Responsive reading

WE DEPART TO SERVE GOD

Scripture reading
Chorus
Benediction
Postlude

WE PRAISE OUR LORD

Prelude
Call to worship
Invocation
Concerns of the church
Hymn of praise

WE AFFIRM OUR FAITH

Affirmation of faith
Hymn

WE CONFESS OUR SIN

Prayer of confession
Affirmation of forgiveness

WE OFFER OUR GIFTS

Offertory hymn
Offering

WE HEAR GOD'S WORD

Scripture reading
Solo
Sermon

WE RESPOND TO GOD'S CALL

Invitation
Benediction
Postlude

THE ORDINANCE OF BAPTISM

Prelude
Hymn
Baptism
Affirmation of faith
Chorus

OPPORTUNITIES OF SERVICE

Concerns of the church
Offertory hymn
Offering

THE ORDINANCE OF THE LORD'S SUPPER

Solo
Sermon
Responsive reading
Prayer of confession
Discipline of silence
The Lord's Prayer
Hymn
The Lord's Supper

OPPORTUNITY OF COMMITMENT

Invitation
Benediction
Postlude

Endless possibilities exist for this type of worship outline. Consider these last two examples. Try completing these outlines for a worship service with your congregation.

WE ADORE OUR LORD
WE CONFESS OUR SIN
WE AFFIRM OUR FAITH
WE DEDICATE OUR LIFE

WE REACH UPWARD
WE REACH INWARD
WE REACH OUTWARD

OUTLINES FOR SPECIAL OCCASIONS

Worship outlines can be created for special occasions. Jewish and Christian worship has always had special days and seasons of worship. In the Old Testament, there were times for special celebration and worship. In Deuteronomy 16:1-17, there is a festal calendar. Instructions are given for special times of worship. Included in this passage are directions for observing the Passover and the Feast of Unleavened Bread, the Feast of Weeks, and the Feast of Booths. Jewish worship has an appreciation for special times of worship.

The Christian church has also developed special worship occasions. We celebrate Advent, Christmas, Easter, and other special seasons and days of worship. In my denomination, little attention has been given to the church year. I have not experimented much with planning worship around the church calendar. I am intrigued by the possibility, however, and may do so in the future. Creative and meaningful worship services could be developed around the Christian calendar of Advent, Christmas, Epiphany, Lent, Holy Week, Easter, Pentecost, and Trinity season. I will leave that task to someone more experienced in following the church year. What follows, however, are examples of worship services constructed around special seasons and days.

For the Christmas season (Advent) last year we used the carol "Joy to the World" as the basis for our order of worship. The first stanza of this hymn works well as a worship outline. Under the phrase "Joy to the World," a time of praise is appropriate. Under "The Lord Is Come," prayer is observed. The Lord comes to us through the experience of prayer. When Christ was born, the Wise Men received Him with gifts. The offering fits well under "Let Earth Receive Her King." As we listen to God's Word, we can prepare room for Him in our hearts. The sermon, then, fits well under "Let Every Heart Prepare Him Room." As we made decisions for Christ, we find celebration and joy. "And Heaven and Nature Sing" is a good place for the invitation and benediction.

JOY TO THE WORLD
Prelude
Call to worship
Worship theme interpretation
Invocation
Concerns of the church
Hymn

THE LORD IS COME
Discipline of silence
The Lord's Prayer
Chorus

LET EARTH RECEIVE HER KING
Offertory hymn
Offering

LET EVERY HEART PREPARE HIM ROOM
Scripture reading
Anthem
Sermon

AND HEAVEN AND NATURE SING
Invitation
Benediction
Postlude

Sometime ago, several of my peers had a "Loyalty Day" at their church. Its purpose was to emphasize the importance of being loyal to Christ's church. Part of the emphasis was to have high attendance and high offering. It was a good way to catch up with the budget! In every case it worked well. We tried it at my church, and it was more successful than we dreamed possible. It was the greatest one-day offering in the history of our church. Here is the worship outline put together for that special day.

LOYALTY DAY

"Let not loyalty and faithfulness forsake you;
bind them about your neck,
write them on the tablet of your heart" (Prov. 3:3).

LOYALTY EXPRESSED THROUGH PRAISE

Prelude
Call to worship
Responsive reading
Hymn
Welcome

LOYALTY EXPRESSED THROUGH PRAYER

Hymn
Discipline of silence
Pastoral prayer

LOYALTY EXPRESSED THROUGH TESTIMONY

Testimony
Solo
Testimony

LOYALTY EXPRESSED THROUGH PROCLAMATION

Anthem
Sermon
Invitation

LOYALTY EXPRESSED THROUGH GIVING

Offertory hymn
Offering
Benediction
Postlude

For Mother's Day or Father's Day, consider this outline based on the hymn "God Give Us Christian Homes." This one is for Mother's Day.

GOD GIVE US CHRISTIAN HOMES!

Prelude
Call to worship
Invocation
Child dedication
Hymn

HOMES WHERE THE MOTHER, IN QUEENLY QUEST, STRIVES TO SHOW OTHERS THY WAY IS BEST

Recognition of mothers
Testimony from a mother
Offertory hymn
Offering

HOMES WHERE THE BIBLE IS LOVED AND TAUGHT

Solo
Scripture readings on the family
Pastoral prayer

HOMES WHERE THE MASTER'S WILL IS SOUGHT

Anthem
Sermon on the home
Invitation
Benediction
Postlude

The same hymn can be adapted for Father's Day.

GOD GIVE US CHRISTIAN HOMES!
HOMES WHERE THE FATHER IS TRUE AND STRONG
HOMES WHERE THE BIBLE IS LOVED AND TAUGHT
HOMES WHERE THE MASTER'S WILL IS SOUGHT

This outline could be used for a Thanksgiving worship service.

THANKING GOD THROUGH PRAISE
Prelude
Call to worship
Hymn
Invocation

THANKING GOD THROUGH PRAYER
Solo
Discipline of silence
Prayer of thanksgiving

THANKING GOD THROUGH GIVING
Offertory hymn
Prayer of dedication
Offering

THANKING GOD THROUGH PROCLAMATION
Scripture readings
Anthem
Sermon or drama

THANKING GOD THROUGH COMMITMENT
Invitation
Affirmation of faith
Doxology
Benediction
Postlude

My denomination has a day on the calendar called "Senior Adult Day." It is an opportunity to affirm the value of senior adults. We decided to observe it in our church. It turned out to be one of the best worship services of the year. The outline was developed from Psalm 92.

IT IS GOOD TO SING PRAISES TO THE LORD (v. 1)

Prelude
Choral call to worship by senior adult choir
Hymn
Invocation by a senior adult
Concerns of the church

TO DECLARE GOD'S STEADFAST LOVE AND FAITHFULNESS (v. 2)

Responsive reading based on verses dealing with aging
Hymn
Testimony by a senior adult
Offering hymn
Offering

THEY STILL BRING FORTH FRUIT IN OLD AGE (v. 14)

Scripture reading by a senior adult
Anthem by senior adult choir
Sermon on the theme
Invitation
Benediction
Postlude

Not long ago our church observed its seventy-fifth anniversary. We decided to throw a party! We had a homecoming and birthday celebration. We used the following outline for the morning worship service.

SEVENTY-FIVE YEARS OF PRAISE

Prelude
Choral call to worship
Invocation
Chorus
Recognition of charter members
Hymn

SEVENTY-FIVE YEARS OF PRAYER

Discipline of silence
Pastoral prayer
The Lord's Prayer

SEVENTY-FIVE YEARS OF STEWARDSHIP

Offering hymn
Offertory prayer
Offering

SEVENTY-FIVE YEARS OF PROCLAMATION

Children's sermon
Scripture reading
Anthem
Sermon

SEVENTY-FIVE YEARS OF SERVICE

Invitation
Affirmation of faith
Benediction
Postlude

   Worship outlines can also be created for a special emphasis. Not
long ago our church put together a statement of purpose. It is important for a church to know why it exists. When it catches a vision
of its mission, it can then be intentional in carrying it out. We came
up with five major purposes as a church. Our objectives were to be
(1) a worshiping congregation, (2) a witnessing partnership, (3) a
caring community, (4) an equipping center, and (5) a loving fellowship. After these were adopted by the church, we decided to develop a series of worship services around them. They were helpful in
interpretating the mission of our church to the congregation. Here is
the outline we used for those five weeks.

Our objective is to be a Worshiping Congregation. God has called His church to engage in personal and corporate worship. Jesus taught us to "worship the Father in spirit and truth" (John 4:23).

PREPARING FOR OUR MISSION

Prelude
Call to worship
Responsive reading
Hymn
Invocation
Concerns of the church

PRAYING FOR OUR MISSION

Chorus
Discipline of silence
Pastoral prayer

SUPPORTING OUR MISSION

Offertory hymn
Offertory prayer
Offering

INTERPRETING OUR MISSION

Children's sermon
Scripture reading
Solo
Sermon

COMMITTING OURSELVES TO MISSION

Invitation
Benediction
Postlude

(Note: the objective printed at the top of the order of worship changed each week. See chapter 3 for the complete worship series.)

Our congregation has enjoyed this approach to worship planning. It has several benefits. First, it helps people better understand and experience worship. Second, it provides variety. If we do not change the order of worship fairly often, it can become too predictable and get into a dull rut. Third, it is a challenging and stimulating exercise for the worship leader. I think you will find great enjoyment in this approach. The end result will be more effective and meaningful worship services.

When we have a worship outline constructed, we are well on our way to getting ready for Sunday. The next step is to fill in the outline with various elements of worship. This is the subject of chapter 2.

2

Filling in the Outline

A worship outline is like a skeleton. While it's essential, much more is needed to sustain life. Once the worship outline is completed, it is time to fill it in with elements of worship. The elements of worship are the vehicles through which God's people worship. This chapter will suggest how you can use them to develop more meaningful worship services.

In this chapter, various elements of worship will be discussed. Several examples will be given of each. Before examining the specific elements, let us see the part they have played in Scripture and church history. This will give us a better foundation on which to stand.

The elements of worship are fairly similar in the Old and New Testaments. In his book *Worship in Ancient Israel*, H. H. Rowley pointed out that Old Testament worship consisted of such elements as adoration and praise, thanksgiving, confession, petition and intercession, and surrender. The forms of worship used in the synagogue included the reciting of the Shema, prayers, Scripture readings, exposition, and blessing.[1]

The New Testament church adopted many of the Jewish elements of worship. They also added new ones. In his book *Jubilate!* Don Hustad offered an overview of the New Testament elements of worship.

The New Christian Synagogue
(Service of the Word)

Scripture readings (especially the prophets, and including letters from Paul): "Till I come, attend to the public reading of scripture" (1 Tim. 4:13). "And when this letter has been read among you, have it read also in the church of the Laodiceans" (Col. 4:16).

Homily (exposition): "On the first day of the week, when we were gathered together to break bread, Paul talked with them . . . and he prolonged his speech until midnight" (Acts 20:7).

A Confession of Faith: "Take hold of the eternal life to which you were called when you made the good confession in the presence of many witnesses" (1 Tim. 6:12). The earliest form of an actual creed may have been as simple as "Jesus Christ is Lord," similar to the Ethiopian eunuch's confession, "I believe that Jesus Christ is the Son of God" (Acts 8:37, KJV).

Singing (of various types): "Psalms and hymns and spiritual songs" (Col. 3:16), probably without instrumental accompaniment.

Prayers: "And they devoted themselves to . . . prayers" (Acts 2:42).

Congregational Amen: "How can any one in the position of an outsider say 'Amen' to your thanksgiving when he does not know what you are saying?" (1 Cor. 14:16).

Collection (alms): "Now concerning the contributions for the saints . . . on the first day of every week, each of you is to put something aside and store it up, as he may prosper, so that contributions need not be made when I come" (1 Cor. 16:1-2).

Physical Action: "I desire then that in every place the men should pray, lifting holy hands" (1 Tim. 2:8).

The Continuing Upper Room
(Service of the Table)

Thanksgiving (eucharist): "And he took bread, and when he had given thanks" (Luke 22:19).

Remembrance (*anamnesis,* Gr.): "Do this, as often as you drink it, in remembrance of me" (1 Cor. 11:25).

The Anticipation of Christ's Return: "For as often as you eat this bread and drink the cup, you proclaim the Lord's death until he comes" (1 Cor. 11:26).

Intercession (following the example of Christ in the Upper Room): "When Jesus had spoken these words, he lifted up his eyes to heaven and said . . . I am not praying for the world but for those whom thou has given me" (John 17:1*a*,9*b*).

The Kiss of Peace (evidently a Jewish practice, continued by early Christians): "So if you are offering your gift at the altar, and there remember that your brother has something against you, leave your gift there before the altar and go; first be reconciled to your brother" (Matt. 5:23-24). (The phrase "kiss of love" or "holy kiss" is found in Rom. 16:16, 1 Cor. 16:20, 1 Thess. 5:26, and 1 Pet. 5:14).[2]

Through the centuries the Christian church has used and adapted these biblical elements of worship. In his book *Christian Worship*, Franklin Segler offers several historical examples.

Justin Martyr described Christian worship in AD 140.

(1) *The Reading of Scripture.*—On the day which is called Sunday we have a common assembly of all who live in the cities or in the out-lying districts, and the memoirs of the Apostles or the writings of the Prophets are read, as long as there is time.

(2) *The Address of the President.*—Then, when the reader has finished, the president of the assembly verbally admonishes and invites all to imitate such examples of virtue.

(3) *The Prayer.*—Then we all stand up together and offer up our prayers, and as we said before, after we finish our prayers, bread and wine and water are presented.

(4) *Thanksgiving and Amen of the People.*—He who presides likewise offers up prayers and thanksgivings, to the best of his ability, and the people express their approval by saying "Amen."

(5) *Distribution of the Bread and the Wine.*—The Eucharistic elements are distributed and consumed by those present, and to those who are absent they are sent through the deacons.

(6) *Collection for the Poor.*—The wealthy, if they wish, contribute whatever they desire, and the collection is placed in the custody of the president. (With it) he helps the orphans and widows, those who are needy because of sickness or any other reason, and the captives and strangers in our midst; in short, he takes care of all those in need.[3]

Let us now examine an example of worship from the time of the Reformation. Calvin's Genevan Service Book has been used as a model of worship by many churches through the centuries. The order of worship used by Calvin in Geneva follows:

The Liturgy of the Word
Scripture Sentence: Psalm cxxiv, 8
Confession of sins
Prayer for pardon
Metrical Psalm
Collection for Illumination
Lection
Sermon

The Liturgy of the Upper Room
Collection of alms
Intercessions
Lord's Prayer in long paraphrase
Preparation of elements while Apostle's Creed sung
Words of Institution
Exhortation
Consecration prayer
Fraction
Delivery
Communion, while psalm or Scriptures read
Post-communion collect
Aaronic Blessing.[4]

The worship pattern of General Baptists in England in 1609 is described below.

The order of the worship and government of our church is: (1) We begin with a prayer, (2) after read some one or two chapters of the Bible; (3) give the sense thereof and confer upon the same; (4) that done, we lay aside our books and after a solemn prayer made by the first speaker (5) he propoundeth some text out of the scripture and prophesieth out of the same by the space of an hour or three quarters of an hour. (6) After him standeth up a second speaker and prophesieth out of the said text the like time and space, sometimes more, sometimes less. (7) After him, the third, the fourth, the fifth etc., as the time will give leave. (8) Then the first speaker concludeth with prayer as he began with prayer, (9) with an exhortation to contribution to the poor, which (10) collection being made is also concluded with prayer. This morning exercise begins at eight of the clock and continueth unto twelve of the clock. The like course of exercise is observed in the afternoon from two of the clock unto five or six of the clock. Last of all the execution of the government of the Church is handled.[5]

The next time your church members complain about getting out a few minutes late, read them the above example! It is interesting to discover that the elements of worship we use today are similar to those found in the Old and New Testaments, and throughout centuries of church history.

With these few biblical and historical examples behind, let us move on to a discussion of the specific elements of worship. The following will be addressed: the call to worship, the invocation, the greeting, Scripture reading, prayer, discipline of silence, the offering, the sermon, music in worship, affirmation of faith, call to commitment, the benediction, and the announcements. Examples will be given of each. Not every element of worship will be considered here. For example, I have left out baptism and the Lord's Supper. That does not mean they are unimportant. On the contrary, they are two of the most significant elements of worship. It is beyond the scope of this book, however, to deal with them. They require a much more thorough discussion than I can provide here. Entire books are dedicated to the Supper and baptism. I would recommend you read such books if you want further insight into observing these two elements of worship.

THE CALL TO WORSHIP

How we begin a worship service is extremely important. The beginning of the service sets the tone for the entire worship event. The beginning of the service is usually referred to as the call to worship. It should be God centered. We come to worship our Lord and praise Him for His greatness. The focus of our worship is the transcendent God. He is worthy of our worship. The call to worship turns our attention to the glory of the living Lord. It should usually be done in a spirit of celebration. Psalm 100 is an excellent example. It could serve as a good call to worship.

> Make a joyful noise unto the Lord, all the lands!
>> Serve the Lord with gladness!
>> Come into his presence with singing!
> Know that the Lord is God!
>> It is he that made us, and we are his;
>> we are his people, and the sheep of his pasture.
> Enter his gates with thanksgiving,
>> and his courts with praise!
>> Give thanks to him, bless his name!
> For the Lord is good;
>> his steadfast love endures for ever,
>> and his faithfulness to all generations.

There are two basic ways to do a call to worship—verbally or musically. Both offer a rich variety of possibilities. Various examples follow.

A responsive reading serves well as a call to worship. It is an effective way to call ourselves to attention and begin worshiping God. The hymnal has many possibilities. We can, however, create our own. Usually they will be based on Scripture passages. Here are some examples, mostly from the Psalms.

Leader: I will bless the Lord at all times;
People: His praise shall continually be in my mouth.
Leader: O magnify the Lord with me,
People: Let us exalt His name together! (from. Ps. 34).

Leader: O come, let us sing to the Lord;
People: Let us make a joyful noise to the rock of our salvation!
Leader: Let us come into His presence with thanksgiving;
People: Let us make a joyful noise to Him with songs of praise!
Leader: For the Lord is a great God,
People: And a great King above all gods.
   All: O come, let us sing to the Lord (from Ps. 95)

Leader: Hear the good news of Easter.
People: Jesus, our Lord, is risen.
Leader: Christ is risen from the dead.
People: Christ is risen indeed!
   All: We worship the Lord who lives.

Leader: Why are we here today?
People: We are here to worship God.
Leader: And why do we worship God?
People: Because He is worthy of our worship.
Leader: Why is He worthy?
People: He created the heavens and earth.
       He gave us the gift of life.
       He provides all our needs.
       He makes us whole through Christ.
       He makes us a community of faith.
       He gives us purpose and meaning.
       He is the one and holy God.
Leader: Yes, God is worthy of our worship.
   All: Let the worship begin!

Leader: O sing to the Lord a new song; sing to the Lord, all the earth!

People: Sing to the Lord, bless his name; tell of his salvation from day to day.

Leader: Declare his glory among the nations, his marvelous works among all the peoples!

People: For great is the Lord, and greatly to be praised.

Leader: O sing to the Lord a new song;

People: Sing to the Lord, all the earth! (from Ps. 96).

Leader: O sing to the Lord a new song,

People: For he has done marvelous things!

Leader: Make a joyful noise to the Lord, all the earth;

People: Break forth into joyous songs and sing praises!

Leader: Make a joyful noise before the King, the Lord! (from Ps. 98).

Leader: Praise the Lord! Praise, O servants of the Lord, praise the name of the Lord!

People: Blessed be the name of the Lord from this time forth and for evermore!

Leader: From the rising of the sun to its setting, the name of the Lord is to be praised!

People: The Lord is high above all nations, and his glory above the heavens!

Leader: Praise the Lord! Praise, O servants of the Lord,

All: Praise the name of the Lord! (from Ps. 113).

Leader: I will extol thee, my God and my King, and bless thy name for ever and ever.

People: Every day I will bless thee, and praise thy name for ever and for ever.

All: Great is the Lord, and greatly to be praised,

Leader: His greatness is unsearchable.

All: Praise ye the Lord (from Ps. 145).

Leader: Praise the Lord! Praise the Lord from the heavens, praise him in the heights!

People: Praise him, all his angels, praise him, all his host!

Leader: Praise him his sun and moon, praise him, all you shining stars!

People: Praise him, you highest heavens,

Leader: and you waters above the heavens!

All: Let them praise the name of the Lord! (from Ps. 148).

A variation of this approach is to do a three-part call to worship using the choir, the leader, and the congregation. This works well, but you must remember to give careful instructions at first until they catch on. Here are two examples:

Leader: This is the day which the Lord hath made;
People: We will rejoice and be glad in it.
 Choir: Enter into his gates with thanksgiving, and into his courts with praise:
People: Be thankful unto him, and bless his name.
Leader: For the Lord is good; his mercy is everlasting;
   All: Come, let us worship the Lord (from Ps. 118 and Ps. 100, KJV).

Leader: O come, let us worship and bow down,
People: Let us kneel before the Lord, our Maker.
 Choir: For he is our God,
People: And we are the people of His pasture,
 Choir: and the sheep of His hand.
Leader: O come, let us worship and bow down,
   All: Let us kneel before the Lord, our Maker! (from Ps. 95).

There are other variations as well. Try having the leader read, then the right side of the sanctuary, then the left side. You could also split the reading between the leader, the men, and the women. This adds variety and excitement as we prepare to worship God through the call to worship.

Of course, there are other possible calls to worship. One person can simply read an appropriate passage. The Psalms provide many such passages.

Praise the Lord! For it is good to sing praises to our God; for he is gracious, and a song of praise is seemly (Ps. 147:1).

I was glad when they said to me, "Let us go to the house of the Lord!" (Ps. 122:1).

This is the day which the Lord hath made; we will rejoice and be glad in it (Ps. 118:24, KJV).

Thousands of verses throughout the Bible could be used as a call to worship. Consider these, all from the Book of Psalms:

81:1
92:1
93:1-2
95:1-7
96:1-9
98:4-6
100
103:1-2
104:1
106:1-2
113:1-4
117
135:1-3
145:10-13
146:1-2
147:1
149:1-2
150

The most natural movement after a verbal call to worship is to sing a song of praise. The invocation fits well after that.

Musical calls to worship are also effective. There are three basic variations. The first is to have a soloist or choir sing a choral call to worship. Another is to have the choir sing the first verse of a hymn and then invite the congregation to sing the remaining verses. A third option is for everyone to sing the Doxology, a chorus, or a hymn of praise. To help create an atmosphere of warmth, have your choir sing "The Bond of Love," then ask everyone to shake hands while the instruments play. After the greeting is over, have everyone sing the first verse of that song. You will find this to be an effective way to begin a warm and dynamic worship service.

THE INVOCATION

The invocation usually follows the call to worship. It should be a brief prayer acknowledging God's presence in the worship service and sensitizing us to His presence. (See the section on prayer for a further discussion of prayer in worship.) The following invocation could serve as a model:

DEAR LORD,
   We know that You are in this place. Help us to worship You today in spirit and in truth. Give us the eyes to see You and the ears to hear You, through Jesus Christ our Lord, in whose name we pray. Amen.

THE GREETING

Years ago I preached a week of revival services at a small country church. At the beginning of each service, the people took a few minutes to shake hands and greet one another. This greeting generated a vibrant atmosphere of warmth and celebration. It was a reminder that we had gathered not only as individuals, but as a community of faith.

The next Sunday I tried it at my church. The congregation responded positively to this time of greeting. It soon became a new tradition for us. Since then, I have incorporated this greeting into my ongoing worship planning and leadership. It is exciting to look out in the congregation and see people greet one another in such a warm and sensitive way. It is an especially good symbol to visitors. This time of greeting adds a positive dimension to a worship service.

Although I liked this approach and was doing it on a regular basis, I had no idea that it had biblical and historical roots. I was excited when I learned that the church had been doing this for centuries.

In Romans 16:15-16, Paul spoke about greeting the saints. He said in verse 16, "Greet one another with a holy kiss." In 1 Peter 5:16, we read, "Greet one another with the kiss of love." In 1 Corinthians 16:20, Paul said, "Greet one another with a holy kiss." He said the same in 2 Corinthians 13:12. In 1 Thessalonians 5:26, we read, "Greet all the brethren with a holy kiss."

This greeting became a part of early Christian worship. We would do well to incorporate it into modern Christian worship. Many churches do this on a regular basis. I learned from Catholic and Episcopalian friends that they observe this greeting, or "kiss of peace" as they call it, every week during their worship services.

Times and culture change, however, and we need to adjust to those changes. While the ancient greeting was a kiss, today it is a handshake. Rather than encouraging your congregation to kiss one another (some would violently object, others would like it!), simply have them greet one another with a handshake. Since customs of greetings have changed, a handshake today is the same as the "holy kiss" of ancient days.

There are many good arguments for observing the greeting in Christian worship. First, it is biblical. That is a good enough reason in itself. Second, it is part of our Christian heritage. The church has been doing this for centuries. The modern church needs to learn from its history. Third, it is an important symbol. It tells us that when we gather together for public worship we come as a community. We are not lone-ranger Christians. We are part of the family of faith. When we observe the greeting in my church, I often say something like this: "We have come today to worship God. We come not only as individuals but as a community of faith. Let us celebrate being the family of God. Take a moment now to greet one another in the name of the Lord."

A fourth reason for observing the greeting is that it adds a positive dynamic to the worship service. A special spirit is generated by this "holy kiss." It adds warmth and dynamism to the worship service. Another reason for observing the greeting is that it meets the needs of people. An elderly widow once told me that the greeting was one of the few times in the week when she experienced human touch. It meant much to her. For these reasons and more, we would do well to have a time of greeting in our worship services.

SCRIPTURE READING

The reading of Scripture has been an important element of worship since Old Testament times. In the eighth chapter of Nehemiah, Ezra read the Scriptures to the people of God. It was a significant event. The reading of God's Word had a strong impact on the people.

In Luke 4:16-22, we read that Jesus went to the synagogue for worship. The central focus of the service was the reading of Scripture. Jesus read the Bible, and then discussed it with the people.

In 1 Timothy 4:13, Paul said to Timothy, "Till I come, attend to the public reading of scripture." The public reading of Scripture has long been a central element of worship in the Christian church.

Christians claim to be people of the Bible. The problem, however, is that we sometimes use little of the Bible in our worship services. In some cases, the only Scripture read is the sermon text. Those of us in the evangelical tradition speak much about the importance of Scripture. But in many cases we have neglected Paul's command to "attend to the public reading of scripture." I have been to many evangelical churches where little or no Scripture was read. This trend needs to be stopped. Some suggestions follow on how to use more Scripture in your worship services.

The call to worship is an obvious place to read the Scriptures. Numerous examples have already been given. Responsive readings are another good opportunity to "attend to the public reading of scripture." They have been a part of worship since Old Testament times. In Psalm 124:1 and 129:1, you will notice the phrase, "Let Israel now say." These are early examples of responsive readings. The leader would introduce the reading and then cue the congregation (or choir) to join in. The hymnal has some responsive readings. We can also develop our own. Here are a few examples. The first comes from Matthew 28 and Isaiah 6. Its subject is evangelism.

Leader: Go ye therefore, and teach all nations,
People: Baptizing them in the name of the Father, and of the Son, and of the Holy Spirit.

Leader: Teaching them to observe all things that I have commanded you.

People: **And lo, I am with you always, even unto the end of the world.**

Leader: And I heard the voice of the Lord, saying, whom shall I send, and who will go for us?

People: **Then I said, Here am I, send me.**

This next responsive reading deals with caring ministry. It was inspired by Matthew 25, although not a direct quote of the passage.

Leader: And the Lord says, I am hungry and need some food; I am thirsty and long for a drink; I am a stranger and want a friend; I am naked and need to be clothed; I am sick and would like a visitor; I am in trouble and need someone to help me.

People: **But Lord, when have we seen you in this way?**

Leader: You see me this way in the lives of those who are hungry and thirsty, those who are lonely and naked, those who are sick and in trouble. Look for me there.

People: **O Lord, had we known it was You we would have responded in a more caring way.**

Leader: Then I will forgive your neglect. And I will come again and give you another opportunity to care.

People: **Yes Lord, come again. And help us to see you, and help us to care.**

This next reading could be used to focus attention on confession and forgiveness. It could be used to introduce or conclude a prayer of confession. It is based on Psalm 51.

Leader: Have mercy on me, O God.

People: **According to thy abundant mercy blot out my transgressions.**

Leader: Wash me thoroughly from my iniquity,

People: **And cleanse me from my sin!**

Leader: Purge me with hyssop, and I shall be clean;

People: **Wash me, and I will be whiter than snow.**

Leader: Create in me a clean heart, O God,

People: **And put a new and right spirit within me.**

Leader: Then will I teach transgressors thy ways,

People: **And sinners will return to thee.**

This next responsive reading can be used to celebrate aging and the senior adults in your congregation. We used it for Senior Adult Day in our church. It is based on several biblical passages concerning aging.

Leader: When I am old and gray headed, O God, forsake me not;
People: Until I have shown thy strength to this generation,
Leader: And thy power to everyone that is to come.
People: Gray hair is a crown of splendor;
Leader: It is attained by a righteous life.
People: They still bear fruit in old age; they will stay fresh and green.
Leader: Even to your old age and gray hairs, I am God,
People: I am He who will sustain you.
Leader: I have made you, and I will carry you;
People: I will sustain you, and I will rescue you.
Leader: Gray hair is a crown of splendor.
People: They still bear fruit in old age.

The following responsive reading focuses on Jesus Christ, the Lord. It is based on the well-known passage in Philippians 2:2-11.

Leader: Though he was in the form of God, he did not count equality with God a thing to be grasped,
People: But emptied himself, taking the form of a servant, being born in the likeness of men.
Leader: And being found in human form he humbled himself and became obedient unto death, even death on a cross.
People: Therefore God has highly exalted him and bestowed on him the name which is above every name,
Leader: That at the name of Jesus every knee should bow, in heaven and on earth and under the earth,
All: and every tongue confess that Jesus Christ is Lord, to the glory of God the Father.

Another way to include more Scripture in your worship is to have a place in the order of worship dedicated to the reading of the Bible. You can do this under the title, "The Ministry of the Word." Many churches have an Old Testament and a New Testament reading every week. Some add a reading from the Psalms and the Epistles. A lectionary can help in choosing the Scriptures.

There are a variety of other ways to read Scripture passages in worship. The most obvious is to have one person read it. You might consider having laypersons do this. It gets them involved in the leading of worship, a principle I strongly encourage. We try to have a layperson lead in worship in some way every week.

When one person reads Scripture in worship, it is effective to give an introductory remark reminding the hearers of its authority. One possibility would be to say: "This is the Word of God. Let us have the ears to hear God's Word to us."

During evening worship services, when the atmosphere is more informal, you could invite people to spontaneously read one of their favorite passages of Scripture. This can be meaningful and effective. It helps illustrate how important the Bible is to the people of God.

One person reading the Bible is appropriate and effective. At times, however, it is good to get the entire congregation involved. You can print the passage in the order of worship so that everyone can read it aloud together. This can be most effective. It gets the entire congregation actively involved in reading Scripture. Be sure to print the passage in the order of worship due to the wide diversity of translations people bring with them to church. One way to avoid printing the text in the order of worship is to have pew Bibles. That way, everyone has the same translation.

Another possibility is to read the Scripture passage in a dialogue form. You enlist several people to read various parts of the passage. This works best when the readers take on the part of the different characters in the passage. A narrator may be needed to hold this type of reading together. I saw this done recently at a Good Friday service. The text was John 18—19 on the passion of Christ. Although this requires some extra effort, it has a powerful and dramatic effect. It could certainly be done a few times a year for special occasions or when the text fits this approach especially well.

If you use your imagination, many creative ways will come to mind for using Scripture in worship services. Our children once acted out a biblical text during the children's sermon. The passage was Mark 2:1-12, the story of the paralytic man whose friends lowered him through the roof in front of Jesus.

Instructions were given to the children concerning their parts. One child played Jesus, preaching to the people in the house. Most of them played the crowd, surrounding Jesus. Four children carried a boy playing the paralytic. They used a towel. They brought him to the house, but it was too crowded to get to Jesus. Finally, they managed to get him to Jesus. The boy playing Jesus was told to say, "Rise up, and walk." The child playing the paralytic man did so.

Caution was used in carrying the child on the towel. They only lifted him a few inches from the floor. Rather than lifting him up high and lowering him in front of Jesus, we pretended that part.

Our children loved this mini-drama as did the entire congregation. The best result is that it brought the biblical text to life for the congregation.

These are just a few examples of how to do a better job of attending to the public reading of Scripture. We would do well to seriously consider how we can add more of Holy Scripture to our worship services.

PRAYER

In Acts 2:42 we learn that the early church "devoted themselves to the apostles' teaching and fellowship, to the breaking of bread and the prayers." In Acts 4:31 we read, "And when they had prayed, the place in which they were gathered was shaken; and they were all filled with the Holy Spirit and spoke the word of God with boldness."

Prayer has long been a central element in worship. The traditional forms of prayer are adoration and praise, confession, thanksgiving, petition and intercession, and surrender. When planning worship services today, we should incorporate these into our worship.

The quality of prayer in public worship can be enhanced in many ways. We're familiar with one individual's praying an invocation or pastoral prayer. There are, however, many other alternatives. Consider printing a prayer in the order of worship for the entire congregation to pray together. One possibility is a prayer of confession. The Bible certainly teaches us to confess our sin to God. Several such examples occur in the Scriptures. There is something special about the community of faith praying together a prayer of confession. The creative worship leader will write confessional prayers which are meaningful to their congregation. It's good to have a prayer of confession when you observe the Lord's Supper. This is one way to promote self-examination and spiritual preparation for the Supper. Here is a prayer of confession which would be appropriate in any worship service.

> DEAR LORD,
>   We confess that we have sinned against You in thought, word, and deed. We have not loved You with all our heart and soul, with all our mind and strength, and we have not loved our neighbor as ourselves. We ask You to forgive our sins through Jesus Christ our Lord. Amen.

After a prayer of confession, it is good to have an affirmation of forgiveness. First John 1:9 serves as an excellent example.

> If we confess our sins, he is faithful and just, and will forgive our sins and cleanse us from all unrighteousness.

Since many churches have a prayer of confession every week, I am including several other examples. These were written by Reverend W. W. Williamson, Jr., a Presbyterian minister. Bill is a master at writing meaningful prayers of confession. Here are five examples from his worship services this past year.

God our Father, Your ways are not our ways, neither are Your thoughts our thoughts. Our way is to preserve our interests; Your way is to sacrifice Yourself. Our way is calculating and cautious; Your way is to love without counting the cost. Our way is to seek after status; Your way is that of humility and service. Show us the futility of our way. Take away our pride, and lead us in Your way that leads to life. Amen.

God our Father, we confess to You those times when we have stood in the way of Your gospel. There were times when we could have been an example of Christian life to others but failed to do so. We had opportunities to share Your Word with others, but we were silent. There were occasions when we knew well what You required of us, but we gave in to lower instincts. Forgive us our failure and sin. Have mercy upon us, and transform us into those who reflect your glory, in the name of Christ our Lord. Amen.

God our Father, by Your grace You give us every good thing we need. We confess that we spend our money on that which is not bread and labor for that which does not satisfy. Forgive us for the way we waste Your gifts:
—spending our money on the cheap and frivolous.
—filling our time with idle activities.
—using our talents only to benefit ourselves.
Help us to remember that You have called us to serve and that Your blessings only belong to us when we are willing to give them away, in the name of Jesus. Amen.

God our Father, we confess our failure to love others as You command. When others needed understanding, we came with judgment. When they needed someone to listen, we gave advice. When they needed support, we added to their burden. Take away our self-centeredness that we might love others as we love ourselves. Remake us after the likeness of Jesus Christ, in whose name we pray. Amen.

Great God, Father of our risen Lord, forgive us for contradicting the good news of Easter. We say that Christ has made all things new, but we want to keep things just as they are. We proclaim His resurrection but live as if He were still in the tomb. We hear His promise of new life for us but live as if we must save ourselves. Forgive our lack of faith in Your living presence. Fill us with the praise of Easter, this day and always, for Jesus' sake. Amen.

Bill also does a good job with the affirmation of forgiveness. He titles this "The Assurance of Pardon" in his order of worship. Here are two examples:

Leader: God's way is the way of forgiveness.
People: **He removes our sins and remembers them no more.**
Leader: Through Jesus He offers cleansing and new life.
People: **In the name of Christ, we are forgiven. Amen.**

Leader: If God kept track of our sins,
People: **Who of us could stand?**
Leader: But with the Lord there is mercy,
People: **That we might be forgiven.**
Leader: His forgiveness is offered to all who accept it.
People: **It is offered through Jesus Christ our Lord. Amen.**

In your order of worship, you can also print prayers of praise, thanksgiving, petition, intercession, or surrender. You might consider asking laypersons in your church to write some of these prayers.

Prayers can also be written for special occasions. This was written for our congregation to pray together on our Day of Prayer for World Peace.

DEAR LORD,
We live in a world of war and rumors of war. Forgive us, Lord, for the part we play in contributing to this lack of peace. We pray today for peace. We pray for inner peace within our own hearts and minds. We pray for peace in our relationships with others. We pray for peace between nations throughout the world. Help us to obey Your command to seek peace and be peacemakers. We pray these things in the name of Jesus Christ our Lord, the Prince of peace. Amen.

The offertory prayer is an important time in the worship service. See the section on the offering for a discussion of this prayer.

You can lead your congregation to meaningful prayer through the use of a guided pastoral prayer. Invite them to offer prayers of praise and thanksgiving; then have a period of silence to allow them to do so. Invite them to pray prayers of confession, and give time for that. Next, encourage them to pray prayers of petition and intercession, and give them time to do so. Finally, suggest that they pray prayers of surrender and commitment, offering their lives in the service of God. This guided prayer accomplishes several things. First, it teaches people how to pray. The disciples once came to our Lord and said, "Lord, teach us to pray" (Luke 11:1). This guided prayer is an effective tool for teaching our people how to pray in a balanced, meaningful way. Second, it offers time in the worship service for people to experience personal and not just corporate prayer. This can be a special time for many in the congregation. It also gives some variety to the prayers offered during the worship service.

The use of the Lord's Prayer can be meaningful in public worship. The people know this prayer, so it is not necessary to print it in the order of worship. It is exciting when we pray together the Lord's Prayer. When we do, we are participating in two thousand years of church history, going all the way back to our Lord. Many churches pray the Lord's Prayer every week. We do it once every three to four weeks, usually to conclude a discipline of silence.

DISCIPLINE OF SILENCE

We live in a noisy and busy world. Many people live their lives at a frantic pace. Little time remains for silence, reflection, meditation, and prayer. To have times to "be still, and know that I am God" is therapeutic. The Bible certainly teaches the value of such moments. Habbakuk said, "The Lord is in his holy temple; let all the earth keep silence before him" (2:20). In most of our worship services, we have what we call a "discipline of silence." The congregation is invited to have a time of meditation and personal prayer. The organist plays softly in the background. This keeps the sniffling, coughing, and squirming children from being such a distraction. At first, this may be awkward for your congregation. As they become accustomed to this period of silence, however, it will become a meaningful experience of worship. On occasions when I have left it out, several people told me that they missed it. I would encourage you to try having a discipline of silence in your church.

THE OFFERING

In Psalm 96:8, we read, "Ascribe to the Lord the glory due his name; bring an offering, and come into his courts!"

One of the ways God's people worship Him is through the giving of gifts. In Old Testament times the sacrifice was an important element of worship. In the New Testament church the offering was a regular part of worship. Paul said in 1 Corinthians 16:2, "On the first day of every week, each of you is to put something aside and store it up, as he may prosper." Worship through giving is clearly a biblical principle. It has also been a part of Christian worship through the centuries. We need to educate our church members that the offering is not just a way to pay the church bills. It is an act of worship. Money is important to all of us. When we give of our financial resources sacrifically and with proper motivation, it can be a powerful means of worshiping God.

One of the mistakes many modern churches has made is to collect the offering during Sunday School. While this has several benefits, it takes away from the offering during corporate worship. Perhaps we should consider changing it to the worship hour.

There are several ways to enhance the offering in public worship. Before the offering is taken, say a few words about its importance. Just a brief statement would be adequate. Remind the people how their gifts are used. Tell them some of the specific ministries they support. Remind them that the offering is an important act of worship. You could do this every four to six weeks. A few such remarks can add meaning to the offering.

Another way to enhance the offering is through the use of the Bible. On occasion, read a passage of Scripture about giving immediately before the offering. You could even print the text in your order of worship and have everyone read it together. Numerous passages are appropriate. A comment or two about the passage could also be made. This will help the congregation focus on the significance of the offering.

A third way to improve the offering is through the use of the offertory prayer. In many cases this is done by one individual. It would be helpful to train persons who lead the offertory prayer (usually the ushers), to pray a prayer directly related to the offering and its use in the kingdom of God. The offertory prayer is not the place to pray for the sick, etc.

It is possible for the entire congregation to pray the offertory prayer together. It should be printed in the order of worship. Here are two examples.

GOD OF ALL GIFTS,
   We bring our tithes and offerings as an act of love and worship. Dedicate the giver and gift for service in Your kingdom, in the name of Him who gave His all for us. Amen.

DEAR LORD,
   We acknowledge that all good things come from Thee. We bring our tithes and offerings as an act of worship, commitment, and surrender. Bless these gifts we pray. Use them to proclaim the gospel to our community and throughout the world. In the name of Jesus Christ our Lord we pray. Amen.

THE SERMON

When I was a seminary student, I pastored a small country church. One day after church, our four-year-old son said: "Papa, are you tired? You look tired."

I said, "Yes, Jonathan, I get tired when I preach."

He said, "Yes, I get tired when I listen!"

It is beyond the scope of this book to give serious consideration to sermon preparation or delivery. Many resources are available on this subject. A few remarks concerning the sermon, however, are appropriate.

The sermon is a central element in the worship event. When we preach, we attempt to bring a word from God to our congregation. It is a great privilege and responsibility to proclaim God's Word. We must realize, however, that the sermon is not the only important element in worship. Worship is not just the "preaching service." The sermon is in the context of the entire worship event. The other elements of worship are not just a warm-up for the main event. Every element of worship is vital and has special value and purpose. Although the sermon is central, the other elements of worship are also important. For that reason, we need to spend time not only in sermon preparation but also in preparing the rest of the service.

Try to preach sermons which last about twenty minutes. This has several benefits. It forces the preacher to have a better prepared and structured sermon. Your sermon will be more focused and thus better.

Another value of shorter sermons is that the attention span of the congregation won't last much longer than twenty minutes. At a youth camp one summer, the preacher was preaching an extremely long sermon. About forty-five minutes into the sermon, he said: "I had not planned to preach this sermon tonight. I got it together this afternoon as I walked around the campground."

The layperson next to me whispered, "I wish he had not taken such a long walk!"

A shorter sermon also leaves plenty of time for the other elements of worship. It leaves ample time for a well-balanced order of worship.

Brief sermons are also biblical. Consider the sermon of Jonah. It was short but effective. Jesus usually did His preaching by telling short stories. Even the Sermon on the Mount is not very long. An example of a long sermon is found in Acts 20:7-12. Paul preached so long that a young man named Eutychus nodded off to sleep, fell from a window, and had to be revived!

Preachers love to preach. It is one of the great challenges and joys of pastoral ministry. As important as preaching is, however, it is not the totality of worship but one part of worship. So much for my sermon!

Altering our sermons from time to time is also a good idea. One of the most effective variations is an occasional first-person sermon. This is where the preacher takes on a character of the Bible and tells his story as if he were that character. These sermons, if done well, are usually met with great enthusiasm. If not done too frequently, perhaps only once or twice per year, you will find that a first-person sermon can be extremely effective. It helps the Bible come alive for your congregation. Children especially seem to like this approach. You should be warned, however, that this kind of preaching takes a lot of preparation. It almost has to be done without notes. An example of a first-person sermon is found in the appendix. For further help, see some of the books which are now available on this subject.

Another idea for enhancing your preaching is to have a dialogue session on the sermon. Occasionally, on Sunday nights I invite the congregation to discuss the morning sermon. This allows them to enter into the sermon and give feedback. This has been well received. It's also a good change of pace for the evening service. It lasts about five to ten minutes. Get things started by asking some questions about the morning sermon. These should be prepared beforehand. These questions should be worded to encourage dialogue, not elicit yes-and-no answers. This helps the people to think about the sermon and its implications. Also, if the congregation knows it's coming up that night, they might listen to you a bit more carefully that morning!

One of my favorite cartoons shows a preacher looking at his calendar. It says, "Only four more days until Sunday!" The preacher, with a distressed expression on his face, says, "Oh, Lord, no one warned me about the relentless return of the sabbath."

This cartoon gets to the heart of one of the greatest challenges of the pastorate. How do we produce a fresh sermon or Bible study one to three times per week? Planned preaching is the only answer. A good philosophy would be, do not go to the office on Monday without knowing what you are going to preach that Sunday. The only way to accomplish this is to plan your preaching and teaching schedule.

Most of our sermons fall into one of five major categories. You can plan your preaching around them. The first is *challenge*. We must continually challenge our people. We are to remind them of the demands of the Christian faith. This means the pastor must preach on such things as commitment, renewal, outreach, missions, evangelism, ministry, ethics, and discipleship.

God's people also need to hear sermons of *comfort*. All of us face difficulties and get discouraged. Every Christian has times of struggle, doubt, pain, and crisis. The pastor should bring a word of encouragement, comfort, and hope to God's people. The Bible has many such passages, and preaching is not complete without it. You can do some meaningful pastoral care from the pulpit.

A third category is the *calendar*. Many special days and seasons can guide sermon topics and texts. These include the Christian, national, and denominational calendars. These calendars can give much direction to our preaching.

A fourth area of preaching is special *themes* or *series*. We can preach a series on a particular book of the Bible or on topics of interest and need. The wise preacher will have several series per year as part of his planned preaching schedule.

The last preaching category could be called *spontaneous preaching*. There are times when we feel inspired to preach on a particular topic or text. Special circumstances sometimes influence pulpit planning. These might include a particular crisis or celebration, or a special need or contemporary event which needs addressing. A creative preacher who plans his preaching around these five categories will find that he has more sermon ideas than he has Sundays to preach them.

For the preacher whose well is going dry, let me offer a suggestion. Make a commitment this year to read the Bible from cover to cover. Jot down every sermon idea which comes to mind during your reading, and put it in a file. I did this three years ago, and I have yet to exhaust even half of the sermon ideas.

MUSIC IN WORSHIP

Music plays a vital role in the worship event. Music is the one medium which can be used in every aspect of worship. We can use music to call ourselves to worship, to praise God, to affirm our faith, to confess our sins, to pray various elements of prayer, and to commit ourselves to service.

The Scriptures abound with examples of using music to worship God. Consider the following examples.

Exodus 15:1
Then Moses and the people of Israel sang this song to the Lord, saying.

2 Chronicles 5:13-14
And it was the duty of the trumpeters and singers to make themselves heard in unison in praise and thanksgiving to the Lord, and when the song was raised, with trumpets and cymbals and other musical instruments, in praise to God.

Psalm 92:1
It is good to give thanks to the Lord, to sing praises to thy name, O Most High.

Psalm 95:1-2
O come, let us sing to the Lord; let us make a joyful noise to the rock of our salvation! Let us come into his presence with thanksgiving; let us make a joyful noise to him with songs of praise!

Psalm 96:1-2
O sing to the Lord a new song; sing to the Lord, bless his name; tell of his salvation from day to day.

Psalm 98:1
O sing to the Lord a new song, for he has done marvelous things!

Matthew 26:30
And when they had sung a hymn, they went out to the Mount of Olives.

Luke 1:46-55
The Magnificat of Mary.

Ephesians 5:19
Addressing one another in psalms and hymns and spiritual songs, singing and making melody to the Lord with all your heart.

Colossians 3:16
Let the word of Christ dwell in you richly, teach and admonish one another in all wisdom, and sing psalms and hymns and spiritual songs with thankfulness in your hearts to God.

Revelation 5:9
And they sang a new song, saying . . .

Music has played a significant role in church history. Consider the great reformer Martin Luther. Luther appreciated the significance of music in the worship of God. His opponents once said, "Luther has done us more harm by his songs than by his sermons."[6] Luther himself said:

> Music is a fair and lovely gift of God which has often wakened and moved me to the joy of preaching. . . . Music is a gift of God. Music drives away the devil and makes people gay; they forget thereby all wrath, unchastity, arrogance, and the like. Next after theology I give to music the highest place and the greatest honor. . . . My heart bubbles up and overflows in response to music, which has so often refreshed me and delivered me from dire plagues.[7]

John Wesley was another great figure in leading people to worship God through music. Wesley wrote directions for singing which are still relevant and appropriate for us today.

DIRECTIONS FOR SINGING
I. Learn these tunes before you learn any others; afterwards learn as many as you please.

II. Sing them exactly as they are printed here, without altering or mending them at all; and if you have learned to sing them otherwise, unlearn it as soon as you can.

III. Sing all. See that you join with the congregation as frequently as you can. Let not a slight degree of weakness or weariness hinder you. If it is a cross to you, take it up, and you will find it a blessing.

IV. Sing lustily and with a good courage. Beware of singing as if you were half dead, or half asleep; but lift up your voice with strength. Be no more afraid of your voice now, nor more ashamed of its being heard, than when you sung the songs of Satan.

V. Sing modestly. Do not bawl, so as to be heard above or distinct from the rest of the congregation, that you may not destroy the harmony; but strive to unite your voices together, so as to make one clear melodious sound.

VI. Sing in time. Whatever time is sung be sure to keep with it. Do not run before nor stay behind it; but attend close to the leading voices, and move therewith as exactly as you can; and take care not to sing too slow. This drawling way naturally steals on all who are lazy; and it is high time to drive it out from us, and sing all our tunes just as quick as we did at first.

VII. Above all sing spiritually. Have an eye to God in every word you sing. Aim at pleasing him more than yourself, or any other creature. In order to do this attend strictly to the sense of what you sing, and see that your heart is not carried away with the sound, but offered to God continually; so shall your singing be such as the Lord will approve here, and reward you when he cometh in the clouds of heaven.[8]

Music can be used at any point in the worship service. It serves well as a call to worship. It is an excellent form of praise and adoration. It can call us to prayer or commitment. It helps us to affirm our faith. Music serves these and a host of other good purposes.

Music can be used to conclude a sermon if a particular solo, anthem, or hymn serves as a fitting conclusion. Consider someone singing "People Need the Lord" as a climax to a sermon on outreach and evangelism. Your choir could sing "Because He Lives" to conclude an Easter sermon. Have the entire congregation sing "When I Survey the Wondrous Cross" as the conclusion to a sermon on the death of Christ.

I am fortunate to work with a competent and cooperative music minister. I see us as partners in worship leadership. We spend time together every week to prepare the order of worship. (For an overview of our planning process see the appendix.) I have been amazed and disappointed to learn that many pastors and music leaders do not meet on a regular basis to plan worship. To me, this is imperative. Even if the music minister is a volunteer or works part-time, this needs to be done. The pastor and minister of music are not two different individuals doing their own thing. They are a worship team and must work together. If they do not, the result will be incongruent worship services. Here are two examples.

The special music of the day ended on a note of deep spirituality. It was a powerful message in song which left the congregation in awe of the holiness of God. The preacher, however, had planned to introduce his sermon with an Aggie joke. He knew the mood was wrong, but he didn't know how to get into his sermon without the joke, so he told it. It was awkward for everyone involved.

The anthem of the service was a song about love. It was based on 1 Corinthians 13. It spoke of God's love for us and our love for others. Then the pastor stood and read his sermon text. It came from 1 Samuel 17 and featured the vivid account of David's defeating Goliath and chopping off his head!

The music was warm and well done. The sermon was a good message. But the worship service was hindered because of dissonance between the message of the music and the message of the sermon. Such situations can be avoided if pastor and music leader carefully plan the service.

Although the pastor will sometimes make suggestions as to music possibilities, most of the selections of hymns, choruses, solos, and anthems will be made by the minister of music. This should be done, however, only after the theme and direction of the service have been planned. For best results, long-range planning is required. That way the theme and direction of the worship services are known several weeks and months in advance.

Our music leader occasionally asks the congregation to read a verse of the hymn rather than sing it. This is one way to keep from leaving out that neglected third stanza. Occasionally, our minister of music tells the background of the hymn. Knowing the context of the hymn's origin adds a meaningful dimension to the singing of that hymn.

AFFIRMATION OF FAITH

The congregation needs to verbally affirm their faith. Some churches do this every week by reciting the Apostles' Creed or some other creed. While many churches reject the use of a fixed creed, they certainly have some basic beliefs which all could affirm.

Believers in the early church affirmed their faith by simply saying, "Jesus Christ is Lord." The church has developed many confessions of faith and creeds through the course of church history.

Your own denominational heritage, theology, and practice will guide you concerning the affirmation of faith. Many variations could be developed and used in worship services. In my church we often read together this Trinitarian affirmation of faith.

> We believe in God the Father, Creator, Ruler of all things, the source of all goodness, truth, and love.
>
> We believe in Jesus Christ the Son, God manifest in the flesh, Redeemer and Lord, and ever-living head of the church.
>
> We believe in the Holy Spirit, God ever-present, for guidance, comfort, and strength.
>
> We affirm our faith and commitment to God and pledge anew to love the Lord our God with all our heart, soul, mind, and strength, and to love our neighbor as ourselves.

CALL TO COMMITMENT

The worship of God should have an element of surrender and commitment. After Moses presented the Commandments of God, the people committed themselves to follow them. Exodus 24:3 says, "Moses came and told the people all the words of the Lord and all the ordinances; and all the people answered with one voice, and said, 'All the words which the Lord has spoken we will do.'"

In Joshua 24, Joshua presented God's message to the people. The climax of that event is found in verses 24-25: "And the people said to Joshua, 'The Lord our God we will serve, and his voice we will obey.' So Joshua made a covenant with the people that day, and made statutes and ordinances for them at Shechem."

Isaiah concluded his worship experience with an act of surrender and commitment. Isaiah said, "Here am I, send me." The same sort of dynamic is found in the New Testament. On the day of Pentecost, Peter preached the gospel. When the crowd said, "What shall we do?" Peter said, "Repent, and be baptized every one of you in the name of Jesus Christ" (Acts 2:37-38).

Worship is not complete without an opportunity to surrender our lives to the will of God in service and commitment. This can be done in several ways. The most obvious is to have a public invitation. While this is an excellent way to incorporate this aspect of worship, there are also other ways.

An affirmation of faith can be a means of committing ourselves to God. The benediction can serve as a challenge to serve God as we depart from the worship service. Hymns can serve as a vehicle to surrender our lives to the Lord. Prayer can also call us to commitment. Baptism and the Lord's Supper summons us to discipleship. There are many ways to call forth commitment in the worship service. Make sure to include this important element in your worship planning.

THE BENEDICTION

How should we end a worship service? A common approach is to call on someone to lead a prayer of benediction. There are other options as well. Your choir can sing a choral benediction or the entire congregation can sing a chorus or hymn. Many churches, for example, conclude the observance of the Lord's Supper by singing "Blest Be the Tie." I enjoy concluding the worship service with a pastoral blessing. Here are three of my favorites.

> May the grace of the Lord Jesus Christ, the love of God, and the communion of the Holy Spirit be with you all (2 Cor. 13:14).

> And may the peace of God, which passeth all understanding, keep your hearts and minds through Christ Jesus (Phil. 4:7).

> The Lord bless you and keep you: the Lord make his face to shine upon you; and be gracious to you: The Lord lift up his countenance upon you, and give you peace (Num. 6:24-26).

Numerous scriptural pastoral blessings could be used as a benediction. Consider the following:

Ephesians 3:20-21
Hebrews 13:20-21
1 Peter 5:10-11
Jude 24-25
Revelation 22:21
Romans 12:1-2

THE ANNOUNCEMENTS

Many worship leaders feel that announcements are inappropriate in a worship service. Some worship leaders simply do not give announcements during the service. I tried this once for a few months but gave it up. Sunday morning worship is the largest gathering of the church. Sometimes we need to inform our congregation about something or promote something. We do ours under the title, "Concerns of the Church."

Three things should be kept in mind concerning announcements. First, they should be kept to a minimum. There is no reason to keep announcing Sunday after Sunday what time the evening service is or when the choir meets. Second, make sure to review the announcements before giving them. This will help you give precise announcements without a lot of rambling. Third, try to think of announcements as opportunities for Christian growth and service. You are offering the congregation various ways for them to grow or minister. When you think of announcements in this way, they do not seem so out of place. This understanding has changed my attitude about announcements. They can be appropriate in a worship service.

Another issue is where in the service to place announcements. There is no ideal place. They can be done at the very beginning, but that is not a very inspiring way to begin a worship service. They can be placed at the end of the service, but the people are ready to leave, and that will not be very effective. The other option is during the service. Some feel this interrupts the flow of worship.

We have recently begun giving our announcements three minutes before the worship service begins. This allows the announcements to be given without interfering with the flow of worship. Almost everyone is in the sanctuary at this time. Immediately after the announcements are over the organist begins the prelude. This approach is working well for us.

3

Completed Orders of Worship

In the first chapter, you saw some skeleton worship outlines. In chapter 2, you saw ways to fill in the outline with various elements of worship. This chapter will put both together and show you completed orders of worship. These are some of the orders of worship used in my church over the past year. They will illustrate what I have been discussing in this book. I hope you can use some of these ideas in your own worship services. Mostly, I hope they will serve as grist for the mill in developing your own.

ORDERS OF WORSHIP OUTLINED
FROM BIBLICAL TEXTS

The Worship of God

Isaiah 6:1-8

AN ENCOUNTER WITH THE LIVING GOD

A TIME FOR PRAISE: "I SAW THE LORD, HIGH AND LIFTED UP."

Prelude
Doxology
Invocation
Hymn of Praise .... No. 9
All Creatures of Our God and King
Concerns of the Church

A TIME FOR CONFESSION: "WOE IS ME! FOR I AM UNCLEAN."

Discipline of Silence
Prayer of Confession

> Dear Lord,
> Like Isaiah of old, we stand before You unclean and sinful. Our actions and attitudes often displease You. We are guilty of doing wrong and of not doing good. Have mercy on us and forgive our sins, through Jesus Christ our Lord. Amen.

Affirmation of Forgiveness

> "Behold; your guilt is taken away, and your sin is forgiven" (Isaiah 6:7).

Hymn .... *Grace Greater Than Our Sin* .... No. 164

A TIME FOR HEARING GOD'S WORD: "THEN I HEARD THE VOICE OF THE LORD."

> **Leader:** In the year that King Uzziah died, I saw the Lord sitting upon a throne, high and lifted up.
>
> **People:** And the seraphim said, "Holy, holy, holy is the Lord of hosts. The whole earth is full of his glory."
>
> **Leader:** And the foundations shook at the voice of him who called, and the house was filled with smoke.
>
> **People:** And I said: "Woe is me! For I am lost; for I am a man of unclean lips."
>
> **Leader:** And he said; "Your guilt is taken away, and your sin is forgiven." And I heart the voice of the Lord saying, "Whom shall I send, and who will go for us?"
>
> **People:** Then I said, "Here am I! Send me."

Anthem .... *Because of Who You Are* .... Choir

Sermon .... GOD IS GREAT .... Pastor

A TIME FOR COMMITMENT: "HERE AM I! SEND ME."

Hymn of Invitation .... No. 187
Send Me, O Lord, Send Me

Offering
Benediction
Postlude

The Worship of God

JOB WORSHIPED AND SAID, "BLESSED BE THE NAME OF THE LORD" (Job 1:20-21)

Prelude
Baptismal Service
Hymn . . . . *Praise Him! Praise Him!* . . . . No. 67
Welcome and Concerns of the Church
Chorus . . . . *Praise the Name of Jesus*

> Praise the name of Jesus,
> Praise the name of Jesus.
> He's my Rock, He's my Fortress,
> He's my Deliverer, in Him will I trust.
> Praise the name of Jesus.[1]

HEAR THIS, O JOB; STOP AND CONSIDER THE WONDROUS WORKS OF GOD (Job 37:14)

Scripture Reading . . . . Job 37:1-5

> At this also my heart trembles, and leaps out of its place. Hearken to the thunder of God's voice and the rumbling that comes from his mouth. Under the whole heaven he lets it go, and his lightning to the corners of the earth. After it his voice roars; he thunders with his majestic voice and he does not restrain the lightnings when his voice is heard. God thunders wondrously with his voice; he does great things which we cannot comprehend.

Discipline of Silence

"The Lord is in his holy temple; let all the earth keep silence before him." (Habakkuk 2:20)

Prayer

Hymn . . . . *I Need Thee Every Hour* . . . . No. 379

Offertory

THEN THE LORD ANSWERED JOB OUT OF THE WHIRLWIND (Job 38:1)

Scripture Reading . . . . Job 1:1-3; 13:21

Anthem . . . . *Unfailing Love* . . . . Choir

Sermon . . . . JOB'S FAITH . . . . Pastor

THEN JOB REPLIED, "MY EARS HAVE HEARD, MY EYES HAVE SEEN, THEREFORE I REPENT" (Job 42:5-6)

Hymn . . . . *Softly and Tenderly* . . . . No. 190

Benediction

Postlude

The Worship of God

IF MY PEOPLE, WHICH ARE CALLED BY MY NAME

SHALL HUMBLE THEMSELVES

Prelude
Special Music . . . . *If My People*
Invocation
Responsive Reading

Pastor: O come, let us worship and bow down.
Congregation: Let us kneel before the Lord, our maker.
Choir: For He is our God,
Congregation: And we are the people of His pasture,
Pastor: And the sheep of His hand.
All: O come, let us worship and bow down. Let us kneel before the Lord, our maker.

Hymn . . . . *Joyful, Joyful, We Adore Thee* . . . . No. 31
Welcome and Concerns of the Church
Chorus . . . . *I'll Tell It Now*

I'll tell it now, the word is Jesus,
He's saving love, He's joy and peace;
I'll share, I'll go 'till millions know;
The word is Jesus, He loves us so.

AND PRAY

Discipline of Silence
Pastoral Prayer

AND SEEK MY FACE

Hymn of the Month .... *Revive Us Again* .... No. 263
Offertory Prayer

> Dear Lord,
>   We bring our tithes and offerings as an act of love and worship.
> Dedicate the giver and the gift for service in Your kingdom, in the
> name of Him who gave His all for us. Amen.

Offering
Children's Sermon
Scripture Reading .... Ezekiel 37:1-14
Anthem .... *A Miracle Will Happen Here* .... Choir
Sermon .... CAN THESE BONES LIVE? .... Pastor

AND TURN FROM THEIR WICKED WAYS

Hymn .... *Turn Your Eyes Upon Jesus* .... No. 198
Benediction
Postlude

THEN WILL I HEAR FROM HEAVEN, AND WILL FORGIVE THEIR SIN, AND WILL HEAL THEIR LAND.

The Worship of God

"I AM THE LORD YOUR GOD" (Ex. 20:2).

WORTHY OF OUR PRAISE

Prelude
Call to Worship . . . . *We Have Come into His House*

> We have come into His house,
> And gathered in His name to worship Him.
> We have come into His house,
> And gathered in His name to worship Him.
> We have come into His house,
> And gathered in His name to worship Christ
>   the Lord.
> Worship Him, Christ the Lord.[2]

Scripture Reading

> Make a joyful noise to the Lord, all the lands!
> Serve the Lord with gladness!
> Come into his presence with singing!
> Know that the Lord is God!
> It is he that made us, and we are his;
> We are his people, and the sheep of his pasture.
> Enter his gates with thanksgiving,
> And his courts with praise!
> Give thanks to him, bless his name!
> For the Lord is good;
> His steadfast love endures for ever,
> And his faithfulness to all generations.

The Greeting
The Doxology
Invocation
Welcome and Concerns of the Church

WORTHY OF OUR PRAYER

Hymn . . . . *Praise to the Lord, the Almighty* . . . . No. 10
Discipline of Silence
Pastoral Prayer

WORTHY OF OUR POSSESSIONS

Hymn . . . . *O Worship the King* . . . . No. 30
Offertory Prayer
Offering

AND GOD SPOKE ALL THESE WORDS (Ex. 20:1).

Scripture Reading

Pastor: And God spoke all these words saying,
People: I am the Lord your God,
Pastor: You shall have no other Gods before me.
People: You shall not make for yourself a graven image.
Pastor: You shall not take the name of God in vain.
People: Remember the sabbath day, to keep it holy.
Pastor: Honor your father and your mother.
People: You shall not kill.
Pastor: You shall not commit adultery.
People: You shall not steal.
Pastor: You shall not bear false witness.
People: You shall not covet.
Pastor: And all the people answered together and said,
All: "All that the Lord has spoken we will do."

Special Music . . . . *Guide Me, O Thou Great Jehovah*
Sermon . . . . TOO SMALL A GOD . . . . Pastor
Hymn . . . . *All Creatures of Our God and King* . . . . No. 9
Benediction
Postlude

The Worship of God

MY MOUTH SHALL SHOW FORTH THY PRAISE (Ps. 51:15)

Prelude .... Gwen Moyle
Baptism
Hymn .... *All Hail the Power of Jesus' Name* .... No. 40
Invocation
Concerns of the Church
Hymn .... *His Name Is Wonderful* .... No. 71

ACCORDING TO THY MERCY BLOT OUT MY TRANSGRESSIONS (Ps. 51:1)

Leader: Have mercy on me, O God,
People: According to thy abundant mercy blot out my transgressions.
Leader: Wash me thoroughly from my iniquity,
People: And cleanse me from my sin!
Leader: Purge me with hyssop, and I shall be clean;
People: Wash me, and I will be whiter than snow.
Leader: Create in me a clean heart, O God,
People: And put a new and right spirit within me.
Leader: Then will I teach transgressors thy ways,
People: And sinners will return to thee.

Discipline of Silence
Hymn . . . . *Grace Greater than Our Sin* . . . . No. 164

THEN WILT THOU DELIGHT IN RIGHT SACRIFICES (Ps. 51:19)

Scripture Reading . . . . 1 Corinthians 16:1-2
Hymn . . . . *Something for Thee* . . . . No. 418
Offering

CREATE IN ME A CLEAN HEART (Ps. 51:10)

Solo . . . . *He Set My Life to Music*
Scripture Reading . . . . 2 Samuel 11:1-5
Sermon . . . . DAVID'S DISASTER . . . . Pastor

A BROKEN AND CONTRITE HEART, O GOD, THOU WILT NOT DESPISE (Ps. 51:17)

Invitation Hymn . . . . *Just As I Am* . . . . No. 187
Benediction
Postlude

ORDERS OF WORSHIP OUTLINED FROM HYMNS

The Worship of God

Let us hold fast the confession of our hope without wavering, for he who promised is faithful; and let us consider how to stir up one another to love and good works, not neglecting to meet together, as is the habit of some, but encouraging one another (Heb. 10:23-25).

BRETHREN, WE HAVE MET TO WORSHIP

Prelude
Hymn . . . . *Brethren, We Have Met to Worship* . . . . . . No. 260
Invocation
Concerns of the Church

AND ADORE THE LORD OUR GOD

> Leader: Praise the Lord! Praise the Lord from the heavens, praise him in the heights!
> People: Praise him, all his angels, praise him, all his host!
> Leader: Praise him his sun and moon, praise him all you shining stars!
> People: Praise him you highest heavens, and you waters above the heavens!
> All: Let them praise the name of the Lord!

Hymn of Praise . . . *Come, Thou Almighty King* . . . . No. 2
Offering

WILL YOU PRAY WITH ALL YOUR POWER

Chorus . . . . *Seek Ye First*

> Seek ye first the kingdom of God, and his righteousness; and all these
> things shall be added unto you, alleluia!

Discipline of Silence
Guided Pastoral Prayer

> Prayers of Praise
> Prayers of Thanksgiving
> Prayers of Confession
> Prayers of Petition and Intercession
> Prayers of Surrender

WHILE WE TRY TO PREACH THE WORD

Scripture Reading . . . . Mark 5:21-43
Anthem . . . . *People to People* . . . . Choir
Sermon . . . . THE PRIORITY OF PEOPLE . . . . Pastor
Invitation Hymn . . . *Wherever He Leads I'll Go* . . . . No. 361
Benediction

> The Lord bless you and keep you: The Lord make his face to shine
> upon you; and be gracious to you: The Lord lift up his countenance
> upon you, and give you peace (Num. 6:24-26).

Postlude

The Worship of God

HOLY, HOLY, HOLY! LORD GOD ALMIGHTY

Prelude

> Leader: And Moses said, "I will turn aside and see this great sight, why the bush is not burnt."
> People: God called to him out of the bush, "Moses, Moses!" And he said, "Here am I."
> Leader: Then he said: "Do not come near; put off your shoes from your feet,
> People: For the place on which you are standing is holy ground."
> Leader: And he said, "I am the God of your father, the God of Abraham, the God of Isaac, and the God of Jacob."
> People: And Moses hid his face, for he was afraid to look at God.

Hymn of Praise .... *Holy, Holy, Holy* .... No. 1
Invocation
Concerns of the Church

EARLY IN THE MORNING OUR SONG SHALL RISE TO THEE;

Duet .... *Because of Who You Are*
Hymn .... *God, Our Father, We Adore Thee* .... No. 3
Discipline of Silence
The Lord's Prayer
Offertory Hymn .... No. 8
Praise, My Soul, The King of Heaven
Offering

HOLY, HOLY, HOLY, MERCIFUL AND MIGHTY

Scripture Reading .... Exodus 33:12-23
Anthem .... *My Tribute* .... Choir
Sermon .... THE FACE OF GOD .... Pastor

GOD IN THREE PERSONS, BLESSED TRINITY!

Invitation Hymn .... *I Surrender All* .... No. 347
Affirmation of Faith

> We believe in God, who is like a good father.
> He is near to us, and strong to help us.
> We believe in Jesus Christ, in whom we see God.
> He is for us the way to truth and life.
> We believe in the Holy Spirit, whose life is in us, giving us new life,
> and healing strength for our spirit.
> We believe our faith is a confident trust in the providence and good-
> ness of God.
> We believe our love, is the means by which this faith will be made
> real in our lives.
> By these, we honor God, and best serve our fellowman.

Benediction
Postlude

The Worship of God

JUST AS I AM, WITHOUT ONE PLEA

Charlotte Elliott was mad at herself, her family and God. At thirty-three, when she should have been enjoying radiant health, she had become an invalid. "If God loved me," she complained, "He would not have treated me this way."

This rebellious spirit not only poisoned her heart but put a strain on the life of the entire family. One evening, her father invited Dr. Caesar Malan, noted Swiss minister and musician, to be a guest in their home. Malan was seated at the dinner table with members of the Elliott family when Charlotte gave vent to one of her typical emotional outbursts, condemning God for His cruelty to her, and criticizing her brother as well as her sister and father for their lack of sympathy. Her father, embarrassed at her lack of respect for their distinguished guest, excused himself and left the room with his other children.

Dr. Malan and Charlotte faced each other across the table. He said, "You are tired of yourself, aren't you?" "What do you mean?" she asked angrily. "You are holding to your hate and anger . . . consequently, you have become sour, bitter and resentful." "What is your cure?" she asked. "You need the faith you are trying to despise." An understanding heart, Charlotte unburdened herself. She asked, "If I wanted to become a Christian and find the peace you possess, what would I do?" He said, "You would give yourself to God just as you are now." She said, "I would come to God just as I am?" "Exactly," he replied. Charlotte accepted Christ, and her life was transformed. Fourteen years later, she penned her spiritual autobiography in a seven stanza poem which began:

"Just as I am without one plea, but that thy blood was shed for me, and that thou bidd'st me come to thee, O lamb of God, I come!"

JUST AS I AM WITHOUT ONE PLEA

Prelude

> Leader: All have sinned and fall short of the glory of God.
> People: The wages of sin is death.
> Pastor: Hear the good news!
> People: God will forgive. God will receive us as his children.

Hymn . . . . *Christ Receiveth Sinful Men* . . . . No. 167
Invocation
Concerns of the Church

BUT THAT THY BLOOD WAS SHED FOR ME

Scripture Reading

> Old Testament Reading: Isaiah 53:1-6
> New Testament Reading: Romans 5:8-11

Discipline of Silence
Pastoral Prayer
Hymn . . . . *Alas, and Did My Saviour Bleed* . . . . No. 113
Offering

AND THAT THOU BIDD'ST ME COME TO THEE

Anthem . . . . *At Calvary* . . . . Choir
Sermon . . . . COMING HOME . . . . Pastor

O LAMB OF GOD, I COME! I COME!

Hymn of Invitation . . . . *Just As I Am* . . . . No. 187
Benediction
Postlude

The Worship of God

A MIGHTY FORTRESS IS OUR GOD

Prelude .... Gwen Moyle
Choral Call to Worship .. *A Jubilant Song* .... Choir
The Greeting
Hymn .... *A Mighty Fortress Is Our God* .... No. 37
Invocation
Welcome and Concerns of the Church

A BULWARK NEVER FAILING

Responsive Reading

Pastor: The Lord is my rock, my fortress, in whom I take refuge.
People: Blessed are those who take refuge in him.
Pastor: The Lord is good, a stronghold in the day of trouble.
People: He knows those who take refuge in him.
Pastor: O Lord, my strength and my stronghold,
People: My refuge in the day of trouble,
Pastor: Hide me in the shadow of thy wing.
People: How precious is the steadfast love of God!
Pastor: The children of men take refuge in thee.
All: The Lord is my rock, my fortress, in whom I take refuge.

Chorus . . . . *Praise the Name of Jesus*

> Praise the name of Jesus.
> Praise the name of Jesus.
> He's my Rock, He's my Fortress,
> He's my Deliverer, in Him will I trust.
> Praise the name of Jesus.[1]

Discipline of Silence
Pastoral Prayer
Hymn . . . . *The Solid Rock* . . . . No. 337
Offertory

OUR HELPER HE, AMID THE FLOOD

Scripture Reading . . . . Numbers 35:9-15
Anthem . . . . *Unto Thee O Lord* . . . . Adult Choir
                        Solo, Doris Bedgood
Sermon . . . . CITIES OF REFUGE . . . . Pastor

HIS KINGDOM IS FOREVER

Hymn . . . . *Only Trust Him* . . . . No. 183
The Doxology
Postlude

EVENING WORSHIP 7:00

Prelude . . . . Gwen Moyle
Hymn . . . . *Joyful, Joyful, We Adore Thee* . . . . No. 31
Invocation
Welcome and Concerns of the Church
Hymn Favorites
Offertory
Sermon . . . . Pastor
            THE CHRISTIAN AND ANGER: CONCLUSION
Benediction
Postlude

The Worship of God

FOR THE LIVING OF THESE DAYS

GOD OF GRACE AND GOD OF GLORY

Prelude
Choral Call to Worship .... Choir
The Greeting
Hymn .... *Crown Him with Many Crowns* .... No. 52
Hymn .... *I Will Sing the Wondrous Story* .... No. 55
Invocation
Welcome and Concerns of the Church

ON THY PEOPLE POUR THY POWER

Anthem .... *People Need the Lord* .... Choir
Chorus .... *People Need the Lord*

> People need the Lord, People need the Lord.
> At the end of broken dreams, He's the open door.
> People need the Lord, People need the Lord.
> When will we realize, People need the Lord.[3]

Discipline of Silence
Pastoral Prayer
Hymn .... *God of Grace and God of Glory* .... No. 265
Offertory

120

GRANT US WISDOM FOR THE LIVING OF THESE DAYS

Introduction of Guest Preacher
Scripture Reading .... Ephesians 3:14-21

> Leader: For this reason I bow my knees before the Father, from whom every family in heaven and on earth is named,
> People: That according to the riches of his glory, he may grant you to be strengthened with might, through his Spirit in the inner man,
> Leader: And that Christ may dwell in your hearts through faith; that you, being rooted and grounded in love, may have power to comprehend with all the saints what is the breadth and length and height and depth,
> People: And to know that love of Christ which surpasses knowledge, that you may be filled with all the fulness of God.
> Leader: Now to him who by the power at work within us is able to do far more abundantly than all that we ask or think,
> All: To him be glory in the church and in Christ Jesus to all generations, for ever and ever. Amen.

Special Music .... *Put Jesus First in Your Life*
Sermon .... STRENGTH FOR THE LIVING OF THESE DAYS

GRANT US COURAGE FOR THE FACING OF THIS HOUR

Hymn .... *Just As I Am* .... No. 187
Benediction
Postlude

ORDERS OF WORSHIP OUTLINED
FROM ELEMENTS OF WORSHIP

The Worship of God

WE ENTER TO WORSHIP GOD

Prelude
Call to Worship

> Leader: This is the day that the Lord has made;
> People: I will rejoice and be glad in it.
> Leader: Enter into his gates with thanksgiving and into his courts with praise:
> People: Be thankful unto him and bless his name.
> Leader: For the Lord is good, his mercy is everlasting.
> All: Come, let us worship the Lord.

Hymn of Praise .... No. 10
Praise to the Lord, the Almighty
Invocation
Concerns of the Church
Hymn .... *I Love to Tell the Story* .... No. 461
Anthem .... *You Shall Be Witnesses* .... Choir
Discipline of Silence
Pastoral Prayer

WE OFFER OUR GIFTS TO GOD

Offertory Hymn .... *People to People* .... No. 308
Offering

WE LISTEN TO THE WORD OF GOD

Children's Sermon
Scripture Reading .... John 1:35-46
Sermon .... MAKING FRIENDS FOR CHRIST .... Pastor
Solo .... *People Need the Lord*

WE RESPOND TO THE CALL OF GOD

Hymn of Invitation .... No. 298
Lord, Lay Some Soul Upon My Heart

WE DEPART TO SERVE GOD

Scripture Reading .... Matthew 28:19-20

Go therefore and make disciples of all nations, baptizing them in the
name of the Father and of the Son and of the Holy Spirit, teaching
them to observe all that I have commanded you; and lo, I am with
you always, to the close of the age.

Chorus .... *I'll Tell It Now*

I'll tell it now, the word is Jesus,
He's saving love, He's joy and peace;
I'll share, I'll go 'till millions know;
The word is Jesus, He loves us so.

Benediction
Postlude

The Worship of God

AFFIRMING OUR FAITH

Prelude . . . . Gwen Moyle

Choral Call to Worship . . . . Choir
Have Faith in God

The Greeting

> Leader: Good morning.
> People: Good morning.
> Leader: Who are you?
> People: We are the people of God.
> Leader: Who made you?
> People: God, our Father, made us.
> Leader: Where do you live?
> People: We live in the Father's world.
> Leader: Why are you here?
> People: We are here to worship.
> Leader: Let the worship begin.[4]

Hymn . . . . *Faith Is the Victory* . . . . No. 377

Invocation

Welcome and Concerns of the Church

Chorus . . . . *'Tis So Sweet to Trust in Jesus*

Discipline of Silence

Hymn . . . . *Faith of Our Fathers* . . . . No. 143

Offertory

126

PROCLAIMING OUR FAITH

Scripture Reading

> Pastor: Now faith is the assurance of things hoped for, the conviction of things not seen.
> **People: For by it the men of old received divine approval.**
> Pastor: By faith Abraham obeyed when he was called to go out to a place which he was to receive as an inheritance;
> **People: And he went out, not knowing where he was to go.**
> Pastor: Now the Lord said to Abram, "Go from your country and your kindred and your father's house to the land that I will show you.
> **People: And I will make of you a great nation, and I will bless you, so that you will be a blessing."**
> Pastor: So Abram went, as the Lord had told him.

Anthem . . . . . . *Come, Thou Fount of Every Blessing* . . . . Choir
Sermon . . . . ABRAHAM: FAITH IS BORN . . . . Pastor

LIVING OUT OUR FAITH

Hymn . . . . *When We Walk with the Lord* . . . . No. 409
Benediction

> Leader: I appeal to you therefore, brethren, by the mercies of God.
> **People: To present your bodies as a living sacrifice, holy and acceptable to God.**
> Leader: And I heard the voice of God saying, "Whom shall I send, and who will go for us?"
> **People: Then I said, "Here am I! Send me."**

Choral Benediction
Postlude

The Worship of God

THE MINISTRY OF PRAISE

Prelude
Call to Worship

> Leader: O come let us sing to the Lord;
> People: Let us make a joyful noise to the rock of our salvation.
> Leader: Let us come into His presence with thanksgiving;
> People: Let us make a joyful noise to Him with songs of praise!
> Leader: For the Lord is a great God,
> People: And a great King above all gods.
> All: O come let us sing to the Lord.

Hymn of Praise ...... *O Worship the King* .... No. 30
Invocation
Concerns of the Church

THE MINISTRY OF PRAYER

Hymn .... *Near to the Heart of God* .... No. 354
Discipline of Silence
Guided Pastoral Prayer

THE MINISTRY OF THE WORD

Old Testament Lesson .... Isaiah 53:3-6; Psalm 22:1-2,14-19
New Testament Lesson .... Luke 19:28-40; Mark 15:22-39

THE MINISTRY OF GIVING

Offertory Prayer

Dear Lord,
   We know that all good gifts come from you. At this time we return to You a portion of what you have given us. We ask your blessings on these tithes and offerings. Let them be used for your kingdom's work. Amen.

Offertory Hymn ...... *There Is a Fountain* .... No. 107
Offering

THE MINISTRY OF PROCLAMATION

Solo .... *Were You There?*
Sermon .... THE CRUCIFIED GOD .... Pastor
Hymn of Invitation .... No. 111
When I Survey the Wondrous Cross
Benediction
Postlude

The Worship of God

AN OFFERING OF WORSHIP

AN OFFERING OF PRAISE

Prelude .... Mrs. Gwen Moyle
The Greeting
Call to Worship

> Leader: Then I heard the voices of thousands and thousands, saying with a loud voice,
> People: **"Worthy is the Lamb who was slain,**
> Leader: to receive power and wealth,
> People: **and wisdom and might,**
> Leader: and honor and glory and blessing!" And I heard every creature in heaven and on earth say,
> People: **"To him who sits upon the throne, and to the Lamb, be blessing and honor and glory and might for ever and ever!"**
> Leader: And the four living creatures said, "Amen!" And the elders fell down and worshiped.

Hymn .... *We Gather Together* .... No. 229
Invocation
Welcome and Concerns of the Church

AN OFFERING OF FAITH

Chorus .... *He Is Lord*

Affirmation of Faith

> We believe in the God of fruittime and harvest, who makes the land to bear gifts in its time and fills our tables with the bounty of his hand;
>
> We believe in Jesus Christ his Son, who was the firstfruit of those that slept, and brings us to spiritual tables where our cups are always full;
>
> We believe in the Holy Spirit, who causes us to remember all things for which we are grateful.
>
> As we prepare to partake of the Lord's Supper, we affirm again our faith in God, and we offer our thanks to Him for all his blessings.

Hymn .... *Come, Ye Thankful People, Come* .... No. 233

AN OFFERING OF PRAYER

Prayer of Confession

> Dear Lord:
>
> We confess that we have sinned against You in thought, word, and deed. We have not loved You with all our heart and soul, with all our mind and strength, and we have not loved our neighbor as ourselves. We ask You to forgive our sins through Jesus Christ our Lord. Amen.

Discipline of Silence
The Lord's Prayer

AN OFFERING OF GRATITUDE

Hymn .... *Sing to the Lord of Harvest* .... No. 232
Offering
Scripture Reading .... Luke 24:13-35
Anthem .... *A Hymn of Thanksgiving* .... Choir
Sermon .... KNOWN BY HIS GRATITUDE .... Pastor
THE LORD'S SUPPER
Hymn .... *Now Thank We All Our God* .... No. 234
Choral Benediction
Postlude

The Worship of God

ENCOUNTERING THE LIVING LORD
THROUGH . . .

PRAISE

Prelude
Doxology
Invocation
Hymn of Praise . . . *Come, Thou Almighty King* . . . . No. 2
Concerns of the Church

THANKSGIVING

Leader: O give thanks to the Lord, for he is good.
People: O give thanks to the God of gods,
Leader: O give thanks to the Lord of lords,
People: For his steadfast love endures for ever!
Leader: To him who alone does great wonders,
People: To him who made the heavens,
Leader: To him who spread out the waters,
People: To him who made the sun and moon,
Leader: To him from whom all blessings flow,
People: We offer our thanks.
All: O give thanks to the Lord, for he is good.

Chorus . . . . *God Is So Good*

God is so good . . . .
God answers prayer . . . .
God loves us so . . . .

CONFESSION

"All have sinned and fall short of the glory of God."

Prayer of Confession

Dear Lord,
We confess that we have sinned against You in thought, word, and deed. We have not loved You with all our heart and soul, with all our mind and strength, and we have not loved our neighbor as ourselves. We ask You to forgive our sins through Jesus Christ our Lord. Amen.

Affirmation of Forgiveness .... 1 John 1:9

INTERCESSION AND PETITION

Hymn .... *Sweet Hour of Prayer* .... No. 401
Discipline of Silence
Pastoral Prayer

SURRENDER

Hymn .... *To Worship, Work, and Witness* .... No. 238
Offering
Old Testament Lesson .... Exodus 18:13-27
New Testament Lesson .... 1 Corinthians 3:5-9
Anthem .... *Here Am I, Send Me!* .... Choir
Sermon .... SHARED MINISTRY .... Pastor
Hymn of Invitation .... *Where He Leads Me* .... No. 371
Benediction
Postlude

ORDERS OF WORSHIP OUTLINED
FOR SPECIAL OCCASIONS

The Worship of God

O COME LET US ADORE HIM

JOY TO THE WORLD

"I bring you good tidings of great joy."

Prelude .... Mrs. Gwen Moyle

> Leader: And in that region there were shepherds out in the field, keeping watch over their flock by night.
> People: And an angel of the Lord appeared to them, and the glory of the Lord shone around them, and they were filled with fear.
> Leader: And the angel said to them, "Be not afraid; for behold, I bring you good tidings of great joy."
> People: "For unto you is born this day in the city of David a Saviour, who is Christ the Lord."
> Leader: And suddenly there was with the angel a multitude of the heavenly host praising God and saying,
> People: "Glory to God in the highest, and on earth peace, good will among men!"

Greeting

Hymn .... *Joy to the World* .... No. 88

Invocation

Worship Theme Interpretation

Concerns of the Church

Hymn .... *The First Nowell the Angel Did Say* .... No. 91

THE LORD IS COME

"His name shall be called Emmanuel, which means, God with us."

Chorus . . . . *O Come, Let Us Adore Him*
Discipline of Silence
The Lord's Prayer

LET EARTH RECEIVE HER KING

"Then, opening their treasures, they offered him gifts."

Hymn . . . . *Come, Thou Long Expected Jesus* . . . . No. 79
Offertory

LET EVERY HEART PREPARE HIM ROOM

"Prepare the way of the Lord."

Scripture Reading . . . . Matthew 1:18-25
Children's Sermon
Anthem . . . . *Bethlehem* . . . . Choir
Sermon . . . . Pastor
        THE MANGER PEOPLE: MARY AND JOSEPH

AND HEAVEN AND NATURE SING

"The heavenly host was praising God and saying, 'Glory to God in the highest.'"

Hymn . . . . *The Savior Is Waiting* . . . . No. 182
Choral Benediction
Postlude

The Worship of God

A SERVICE OF THANKSGIVING

THANKING GOD THROUGH PRAISE

Prelude . . . . Handbell Choir
Now Let Us All Praise God and Sing . . . . Choir
Call to Worship

>Leader: Good morning.
>People: Good morning.
>Leader: Who are you?
>People: We are the people of God.
>Leader: Who made you?
>People: God, our Father, made us.
>Leader: Where do you live?
>People: We live in the Father's world.
>Leader: Why are you here?
>People: We are here to worship.
>Leader: Let the worship begin.[5]

Hymn . . . . *We Gather Together* . . . . No. 229
Invocation
Concerns of the Church

THANKING GOD THROUGH PRAYER

Solo
Discipline of Silence . . . . *O Give Thanks to the Lord*
Prayer of Thanksgiving and the Lord's Prayer

THANKING GOD THROUGH GIVING

Hymn .... *Come, Ye Thankful People, Come* .... No. 233
Prayer of Dedication
Offering

THANKING GOD THROUGH PROCLAMATION

Scripture Reading

> Old Testament Lesson: Psalm 136:1-9
> New Testament Lesson: Luke 17:11-19

Anthem .... *A Hymn for Thanksgiving* .... Choir
Sermon .... AN ATTITUDE OF GRATITUDE .... Pastor

THANKING GOD THROUGH COMMITMENT

Invitation Hymn ... *Take My Life, and Let It Be* .... No. 373
Affirmation of Faith

> We believe in God the Father, Creator, Ruler of all things, the
> Source of all goodness, truth, and love.
> We believe in Jesus Christ the Son, God manifest in the flesh,
> Redeemer and Lord, and ever-living Head of the church.
> We believe in the Holy Spirit, God ever-present, for guidance, com-
> fort, and strength.
> We affirm our commitment to God, and pledge anew to love the
> Lord our God with all our heart, soul, mind, and strength, and to
> love our neighbor as ourselves.

Doxology
Benediction
Postlude

The Worship of God

GOD, GIVE US CHRISTIAN HOMES!

Prelude
Doxology
Invocation

Pastor: The Lord God formed man of dust from the ground, and breathed into his nostrils the breath of life;

People: And man became a living being.

Pastor: Then the Lord God said, "It is not good that man should be alone;

People: I will make him a helper fit for him."

Pastor: Then the man said, "This at last is bone of my bones and flesh of my flesh;

People: She shall be called Woman, because she was taken out of Man."

Pastor: So God created man in his own image, in the image of God he created them; male and female he created them.

People: And God blessed them, and God said to them,

Pastor: "Be fruitful and multiply, and fill the earth."

All: And God saw everything he had made, and behold, it was very good.

Hymn . . . . No. 397
Children's Dedication Service

HOMES WHERE THE MOTHER, IN QUEENLY QUEST, STRIVES TO SHOW OTHERS THY WAY IS BEST.

Recognition of Mothers
Scripture Reading .... Proverbs 31:10-11,25-29
Testimony

HOMES WHERE THE BIBLE IS LOVED AND TAUGHT,

Scripture Reading .... Deuteronomy 6:4-7

> Hear, O Israel: The Lord our God is one Lord; and you shall love the Lord your God with all your heart, and with all your soul, and with all your might. And these words which I command you this day shall be upon your heart; and you shall teach them diligently to your children.

Offertory Hymn .... No. 148
Word of God, Across the Ages
Offertory

HOMES WHERE THE MASTER'S WILL IS SOUGHT.

Scripture Reading .... Luke 1; John 19 (selected verses)
Anthem .... *The Gift of Love* .... Choir
Sermon ..... THE BEST SUPPORTING ACTRESS ...... Pastor
Invitation Hymn .... *Jesus Is Tenderly Calling* .... No. 188
Benediction
Postlude

The Worship of God

LOYALTY DAY

"Let not loyalty and faithfulness forsake you, bind them about your neck, write them on the tablet of your heart" (Prov. 3:3).

loy'al-ty, n.: the state or quality of being loyal; faithfulness or faithful adherence to a person, government, cause, duty, etc.

(Webster's Dictionary)

In the beginning, the time being 1910 going into 1911, a town was being born. . . . The town blueprints provided no definite place of worship. But there was a vision. The vision took shape in the hearts of a few members of the First Baptist Church, Helena, and under the leadership of J. M. Porter, they began holding religious services in homes or open air meetings on street corners. The Lord's blessings were on the small group and it grew in numbers and strength. . . . Their faith, their determination, their joy in that day are our heritage.

(History of West Helena Baptist Church)

For seventy-five years, West Helena Baptist Church has served the Lord in this community. It has taken the loyalty of many people to make this possible. Today we affirm our loyalty to Christ, and renew our commitment to serving Him through His church.

LOYALTY EXPRESSED THROUGH PRAISE

Prelude
Choral Call to Worship
Responsive Reading .... No. 522
Hymn .... *The Church's One Foundation* .... No. 236
Concerns of the Church

LOYALTY EXPRESSED THROUGH PRAYER

Hymn .... *Sweet Hour of Prayer* .... No. 401
Discipline of Silence
Pastoral Prayer

LOYALTY EXPRESSED THROUGH TESTIMONY

Testimony
Special Music .... *The Name of Jesus* .... Men's Quartet
Testimony

LOYALTY EXPRESSED THROUGH PROCLAMATION

Anthem .... *He Lifted Me* .... Choir
Sermon .... EXPRESSIONS OF LOYALTY .... Pastor
Invitation Hymn .... *I Surrender All* .... No. 347

LOYALTY EXPRESSED THROUGH GIVING

Offertory Hymn ... *Take My Life, and Let It Be* .... No. 373
Offering
Benediction .... *The Bond of Love* .... No. 259
Postlude

The Worship of God

SENIOR ADULT DAY

IT IS GOOD TO SING PRAISES TO THE LORD (Ps. 92:1)

Prelude

Choral Call to Worship . . . . Senior Adult Choir
Blessed Assurance

The Greeting

Affirmation of Faith

> We believe in God the Father, Creator, Ruler of all things, the Source of all goodness, truth, and love.
>
> We believe in Jesus Christ the Son, God manifest in the flesh, Redeemer and Lord, and ever-living Head of the church.
>
> We believe in the Holy Spirit, God ever-present, for guidance, comfort and strength.
>
> We affirm our commitment to God, and pledge anew to love the Lord our God with all our heart, soul, mind, and strength, and to love our neighbor as ourselves.

Hymn . . . . *How Great Thou Art* . . . . No. 35

Invocation

Welcome and Concerns of the Church

TO DECLARE GOD'S STEADFAST LOVE
AND FAITHFULNESS (Ps. 92:2)

Responsive Reading

Pastor: When I am old and gray headed, O God, forsake me not;
People: Until I have shown thy strength to this generation,
Pastor: And thy power to everyone that is to come.
People: Gray hair is a crown of splendor,
Pastor: It is attained by a righteous life.
People: They still bear fruit in old age, they will stay fresh and green.
Pastor: Even to your old age and gray hairs, I am God,
People: I am He who will sustain you.
Pastor: I have made you and I will carry you;
People: I will sustain you and I will rescue you.
Pastor: Gray hair is a crown of splendor.
All: They still bear fruit in old age.

Hymn . . . . *I Love to Tell the Story* . . . . No. 461
Testimony
Hymn . . . . *Since Jesus Came into My Heart* . . . . No. 487
Offertory

THEY STILL BRING FORTH FRUIT
IN OLD AGE (Ps. 92:14)

Scripture Reading . . . . 1 Kings 3:3-10; 11:4-11
Anthem . . . . *The Longer I Serve Him* . . Senior Adult Choir
Sermon . . . . THE SECOND HALF . . . . Pastor
Hymn . . . . *Living for Jesus* . . . . No. 348
Benediction
Postlude

A WORSHIP SERIES ON THE MISSION OF THE CHURCH

The Worship of God

Our objective is to be a Worshiping Congregation. God has called His church to engage in personal and corporate worship. Jesus taught us to "worship the Father in spirit and truth" (John 4:23).

PREPARING FOR OUR MISSION

Prelude

Choral Call to Worship .... Choir
Now Let Us All Praise God and Sing

Responsive Reading

> Pastor: Why are we here today?
> People: We are here to worship God.
> Pastor: And why do we worship God?
> People: Because He is worthy of our worship.
> Pastor: Why is He worthy?
> People: He created the heavens and earth.
> He gave us the gift of life.
> He provides all our needs.
> He makes us whole through Christ.
> He makes us a community of faith.
> He gives our life purpose and meaning.
> He is the one and holy God.
> Pastor: Yes, God is worthy of our worship.
> All: Let the worship begin!

Hymn .... *Brethren, We Have Met to Worship* ...... No. 260

Invocation

Concerns of the Church

PRAYING FOR OUR MISSION

Discipline of Silence

"Be still, and know that I am God" (Ps. 46:10).

The Lord's Prayer

SUPPORTING OUR MISSION

Hymn .... *Come, Thou Fount of Every Blessing* .... No. 13
Offertory Prayer

God of all gifts, we bring our tithes and our offerings as an act of love and worship. Dedicate the giver and the gift for service in Your kingdom. In the name of Him who gave His all for us. Amen.

Offering

INTERPRETING OUR MISSION

Children's Sermon
Scripture Reading .... Genesis 8:13 to 9:1
Special Music .... *I Saw the Lord*
Message ..... A WORSHIPING CONGREGATION .... Pastor

COMMITTING OURSELVES TO MISSION

Invitation Hymn .... *Just As I Am* .... No. 187
Benediction
Postlude

The Worship of God

Our objective is to be a Witnessing Partnership. The church is to proclaim the good news of the gospel to our community, nation, and throughout the world. Christ commanded His church to "Go therefore and make disciples of all nations" (Matt. 28:19).

PREPARING FOR OUR MISSION

Prelude
Call to Worship .... *I'll Tell It Now*

> I'll tell it now, the word is Jesus,
> He's saving love, He's joy and peace;
> I'll share, I'll go 'till millions know;
> The Word is Jesus, He loves us so.

Invocation
Concerns of the Church
Hymn .... *We've a Story to Tell* .... No. 281
Responsive Reading

> Pastor: Go ye therefore and teach all nations,
> People: Baptizing them in the name of the Father, and of the Son, and of the Holy Spirit.
> Pastor: Teaching them to observe all things that I have commanded you,
> People: And lo, I am with you alway, even unto the end of the world.
> Pastor: And I heard the voice of the Lord, saying, "Whom shall I send, and who will go for us?"
> People: Then I said, "Here am I! Send me."

PRAYING FOR OUR MISSION

Discipline of Silence

> "The Lord is in his holy temple, let all the earth keep silence before him" (Hab. 2:20).

Pastoral Prayer

SUPPORTING OUR MISSION

Hymn . . . . *I Love to Tell the Story* . . . . No. 461
Offertory Prayer

> Our Lord, we acknowledge that all good things come from Thee. We bring our tithes and offerings as an act of worship, commitment, and surrender. Bless these gifts we pray. Use them to proclaim the gospel to our community and throughout the world. In the name of Jesus Christ, our Lord. Amen.

Offering

INTERPRETING OUR MISSION

Children's Sermon
Scripture Reading . . . . Mark 2:1-12
Special Music
Message . . . . . . A WITNESSING PARTNERSHIP . . . . Pastor

COMMITTING OURSELVES TO MISSION

Invitation Hymn . . . . *Set My Soul Afire* . . . . No. 302
Benediction
Postlude

The Worship of God

Our objective is to be a Caring Community. Jesus taught His church by example and words to minister to the physical, emotional, and spiritual needs of people. "So then, as we have opportunity, let us do good to all men" (Gal. 6:10).

PREPARING FOR OUR MISSION

Prelude
Doxology
Invocation
Concerns of the Church
Hymn . . . . *Do You Really Care?* . . . . No. 316
Responsive Reading

> Pastor: And the Lord says, I am hungry and need some food; I am thirsty and long for a drink; I am a stranger and want a friend; I am naked and need to be clothed; I am sick and would like a visitor; I am in trouble and need someone to help me.
>
> People: But Lord, when have we seen You in this way?
>
> Pastor: You see Me this way in the lives of those who are hungry and thirsty, those who are lonely and naked, those who are sick and in trouble. Look for Me there.
>
> People: O Lord, had we known it was You we would have responded in a more caring way.
>
> Pastor: Then I will forgive your neglect. And I will come again and give you another opportunity to care.
>
> People: Yes, Lord, come again. And help us to see You. And help us to care.

PRAYING FOR OUR MISSION

Special Music . . . . *Reach Out and Touch* . . . . Choir
Prayer of Confession

> Dear Lord, You have taught us to reach out and touch. You have asked us to be concerned about people who hurt, and have called us to minister to the physical, emotional, and spiritual needs of others. At times we have done this. Many times we have not. Often we are so self-centered that we neglect the needs of others. Forgive us, Lord. Help us to care more. Help us to see the needs of people. Help us to be a caring community. In the name of Him who gave His all for others, Jesus Christ, our Lord. Amen.

SUPPORTING OUR MISSION

Hymn . . . . *Take My Life, and Let It Be* . . . . No. 373
Offering

INTERPRETING OUR MISSION

Scripture Reading . . . . John 13:1-17
Anthem . . . . *Here Am I, Send Me* . . . . Choir
Sermon . . . . A CARING COMMUNITY . . . . Pastor

COMMITTING OURSELVES TO MISSION

Invitation . . . . *Take My Life, Lead Me, Lord* . . . . No. 366
Benediction
Postlude

The Worship of God

Our objective is to be an Equipping Center. The church is called to equip its people to live as Christians in all areas of life. The scriptures teach us "to equip the saints for the work of ministry" (Eph. 4:12).

PREPARING FOR OUR MISSION

Prelude
Invocation
Choral Call to Worship .... Choir
Come, Christians, Join to Sing
Affirmation of Faith

> We believe in God the Father, Creator, and Ruler of heaven and earth.
> We believe in Jesus Christ His Son, who was crucified for our sin and who rose victoriously from the dead on the third day.
> We believe in the Holy Spirit, God ever-present for guidance, comfort, and strength.

Hymn .... *Come, Thou Almighty King* .... No. 2
Concerns of the Church
Testimony

PRAYING FOR OUR MISSION

Hymn .... *More About Jesus* .... No. 327
Discipline of Silence

> "May the God of peace equip you with everything good for doing His will" (Heb. 13:20-21).

Pastoral Prayer

SUPPORTING OUR MISSION

Hymn .... *To Worship, Work, and Witness* .... No. 238
Offertory

> "And God is able to make all grace abound to you, so that in all
> things at all times, having all that you need, you will abound in
> every good work" (2 Cor. 9:8, NIV).

INTERPRETING OUR MISSION

Children's Sermon
Scripture Reading .... Ephesians 4:7,11-16
Special Music
Message .... AN EQUIPPING CENTER .... Bill Craig

COMMITTING OURSELVES TO MISSION

Hymn .... *Living for Jesus* .... No. 348
Benediction
Postlude

The Worship of God

Our objective is to be a Loving Fellowship. One of the great benefits of being a Christian is the love, encouragement and friendship of the church family. The Bible says, "Beloved, let us love one another" (1 John 4:7).

PREPARING FOR OUR MISSION

Prelude
Call to Worship .... *The Bond of Love* .... Choir
Invocation
Hymn .... *Marching to Zion* .... No. 505
Concerns of the Church

PRAYING FOR OUR MISSION

Testimony
Prayer of Thanksgiving

> Dear Lord, for loving us and adopting us Your children, we are thankful. Thank You for making us one through Jesus Christ. For our life together as a loving fellowship, we are grateful. Help us, Lord, to love You more. Help us to love each other more. Help us to truly be one in the bond of love. Amen.

Meditation .... *Sweet, Sweet Spirit* .... Bill Craig

SUPPORTING OUR MISSION

Hymn .... *Christian Hearts, in Love United* .... No. 253
Offertory

INTERPRETING OUR MISSION

Children's Sermon
Scripture Reading .... Ecclesiastes 4:9-12
Anthem .... *A Common Love* .... Choir
Sermon .... A LOVING FELLOWSHIP .... Pastor

COMMITTING OURSELVES TO OUR MISSION

Invitation .... *He Leadeth Me!* .... No. 218
Benediction .... *Blest Be the Tie*

4

What Others Are Doing

Learning how other worship leaders operate was an enjoyable part of writing this book. None of us has the final word on worship planning. Thus, we have much to learn from one another. Several worship leaders from around the country were asked to contribute to this project. I am grateful for their willingness to participate. They were asked to write a brief overview of their planning processes and to send several orders of worship.

Some of these worship leaders are from large churches; others, from small congregations. The attendance in their worship services ranges from one hundred to over one thousand. They differ in style, theology, and denominational affiliation. Each of them, however, shares two things in common. They are committed to the priority of worship, and they are intentional in their worship planning. Their planning procedures and some sample orders of worship follow. In brief overview, this is how they get ready for Sunday.

DOUG DICKENS
Fort Worth, Texas

[Most of the contributors for this chapter, "What Others Are Doing," are brief and pragmatic—as they were asked. I felt it appropriate, however, to begin the chapter with a longer, more philosophical treatment of the subject. I asked Doug Dickens, professor of Pastoral Ministry at Southwestern Baptist Seminary, to write such an article.

Dr. Dickens is well qualified for this assignment. He teaches worship at the seminary. He also has had many years experience as worship leader in a local church. His reflections, "A Pastor/Professor Thinks About Worship," follows.]

A PASTOR/PROFESSOR THINKS ABOUT WORSHIP

Albert Einstein was once asked what was vital in mathematics. Einstein replied that the blackboard of complicated equations should be erased. "Now, write on the board," he said, "two plus two equals four. That is what is vital in math."

Is it any wonder that so many worship leaders feel frustrated about their worship leadership? Only a small percentage have taken a focused course in worship. Failing to understand the biblical, theological, historical, and psychological essentials of Christian worship, we are like ships without rudders. Subject to every wind and tide of the apparent "vogue," we often run our sails into the breezes of entertainment and slick programming, only to end up on the rocks of the mundane. Many a minister has discovered that he lacks the dollars and expertise to compete with what appears to work for the TV preachers and sometimes superchurch.

Perhaps, apart from the fresh winds of God's Holy Spirit, one of the things we need most as we lead our people in worship from week to week, is a philosophy of worship that guides us in our planning. What follows is an attempt to express the principles which guide me as I lead my congregation in a public discovery of the Divine. This will be followed by some specific examples of worship with my previous congregation, the First Baptist Church of Hot Springs, Arkansas.

WHAT I BELIEVE ABOUT CHRISTIAN WORSHIP

1. *I believe worship is an inevitable dimension of the Christian life*, necessary for the existence and growth of the believer. Worship is to the believer what water is to a fish, or air to an airplane. No meaningful Christian experience is to be had apart from the discipline of worship with fellow disciples.

2. *I believe worship is the disciplined blending of a variety of Christian exercises* into a meaningful experience. The total act of worship is greater than the sum of its parts. Variety has always described meaningful worship. Consider the possibilities: (1) calls to worship and invitations to praise; (2) times for confession of sin, acceptance of forgiveness, and affirmation of faith; (3) awareness of God's goodness to us, an awareness which motivates the grateful to offer his and her best gifts to God; (4) many different kinds of prayers; (5) the reading of sacred Scripture with sermonic application from the Word of God to the world of God; (6) invitation to responsible discipleship; (7) praise through music, testimonies both spoken and sung, and symbolic activities which speak of the marvelous intervention of God in our lives (such as baptism, communion, dedications).

3. *I believe every aspect of worship is sacred and primary, flowing with a purposeful movement towards a new sense of worth and Christian commitment.* Finding its basic meaning in the Anglo-Saxon *weorthscipe*, worship smacks of worth-ship. The sung word of God is as important to me as the spoken word. Usually the most meaningful time of worship for me as a pastor is during the offertory or anthem, times when I am not leading but responding to another's direction to God. All acts of worship (prayers, confessions, hymns, sermon, etc.) should be coordinated and move with unity and purpose toward a challenging application of God's good news for our lives. In worship we find a new sense of worth—a God worth worshiping and serving, a self and life worth living, and others worth caring for and loving.

4. *I believe worship must address the estrangement of our day,* where most persons live without purpose in a joyless, fragmented world. If this is true, even the "passing of the peace," the welcome (or, "expression of Christian friendship," as I call it) becomes an important act of worship. There are significant hopes for this activity: (1) to encourage "outsiders" to feel welcomed by word, smile, and the physical touch of another; (2) to be creative and varied so as not to be monotonous and expected ("Will all the visitors please raise their hands, so we can give you a visitor's card to fill out and drop

in the offering plate?"); (3) to remind even longtime faithful members that we, too, are guests, welcomed by our Heavenly Father in His house; (4) to encourage all those present to participate; and (5) to heighten expectation that no matter how often we have been to this place, something new, dynamic, and life changing should happen to us today.

5. *I believe each prayer is unique and should be designed to serve a specific purpose in the worship experience.* Public prayer is not a private experience, especially when one is leading others in listening to and speaking to God. Invocations should invite. Pastoral prayers should be creative, intercessory, and contemporary. Offertory prayers ought to focus on God's gifts and blessings—and ours—not just another chance for someone to mumble under his breath about "the sick and afflicted," and "all the missionaries on the foreign fields." Moreover, it is the minister's responsibility to see that those who lead in public prayers understand the unique purpose of each prayer and be helped to pray accordingly.

6. *I believe worship culminates in a spoken yet symbolic blessing on God's people as they leave to struggle and serve.* The benediction is one of the most overlooked pastoral tools of the worship arsenal. Clinical psychologist Paul Pruyser, of Menninger's Clinic, both wrote and spoke to ministers years ago about the importance of the benediction as a pastoral blessing. As I understand and utilize this unique prayer, the people do not address God through the pray-er, but rather, God addresses and blesses His people through the raised arms and spoken words of the minister. Thus, the benediction is both verbal, yet visually symbolic, as the minister raises hands to physically bless, on God's behalf, God's people. What a challenging way to "depart to serve."

7. *I believe that worship is both paradoxical and dialectical.* It is corporate, yet intensely personal. It is timeless, yet temporal. It is objective as it focuses on the Creator, yet subjective as it speaks to the created. It is both psychological, yet physical. It is intellectual, yet emotional. Genuine worship must speak to the total person, even as we sit, stand, kneel, walk, touch, hear, taste, and speak.

8. *I believe that public worship should be both spontaneous and planned.* This blending of freedom and form is essential, for liberty and liturgy are the "twin pillars" of worship. It is not only possible but also desirable that worship be both orderly and spontaneous. The emotional level of a given congregation determines the spontaneity of the worship experience. The essentials of unity and purpose in worship are impossible without planning. Great themes of the Christian

faith often may be used as the thread which holds the experience together through hymns, prayers, Scripture, and sermon. In it all, the Spirit of God comes to us in serendipity at this "tent of meeting."

9. *I believe that worship is priestly and also liturgical.* To the uninformed, these are the same. Worship is liturgy, "the work of the people." For Baptists, worship at its best is the involvement of all God's people in the experience. While our worship is usually planned and led by the priestly person, the professional, it must never be understood as a performance by professionals. Kierkegaard's analogy of worship as a drama in which the congregation acts, the priestly leaders prompt, and God serves as the Divine Audience could correct much of our impoverished attempts to meet God.

10. *I believe that worship must be relevant to the personal needs and timely seasons of the Christian faith.* In our reaction to pre-Reformation Catholicism, Baptists seem to be unaware of the "passages" of faith celebrated by Christians around the globe. Not only does the Christian calendar but also the secular calendar provide opportunity for worship to address major issues of life such as work (Labor Day), Family (Mother's and Father's Day), grief (Memorial Day), and Christian and political freedom (Independence Day). How unfortunate that many of our Baptist congregations have not been helped to understand the planning of special worship seasons in the Judeo-Christian tradition. Thus we seldom are led to celebrate meaningfully such great times as Advent, Lent, or Pentecost.

PLANNING AND TEAMWORK IN WORSHIP

Worship does not happen accidentally. For me as a pastor-preacher, a planned program of preaching is essential for worship planning months in advance of any given Sunday. This preaching program allows the minister of music opportunity to coordinate worship music thematically with sermon and Scripture, avoiding frequent repetition of certain hymns while overlooking others.

This kind of planning for public worship calls for time to be calendared weekly with the minister of music in order for adequate creativity and coordination to take place. I found that from one to two hours weekly must be spent with the worship leadership if this happens. This is a shared concern. It is vital to the planning process that ideas be shared by all leaders, and that the pastor-preacher not dictate only what he wants. On the other extreme, some pastors merely "delegate" this worship responsibility to another staff member. Both the dictation and delegation theories are counterproductive.

Regular weekly planning provides opportunity for the ministers to prepare and instruct others who will participate in the shared leadership of worship. These persons include those who will lead in any public prayer, sing, provide instrumental music, etc.

Ultimately, the planning and teamwork of the worship experience unites ministers and congregation. It must regularly be baptized with prayer, willing feedback and evaluation, and a spirit of adventure which commences in the study and culminates in the sanctuary.

I once heard of a Sunday School teacher trying to find a creative way to emphasize the Christmas story, especially the part of the star in the East. She asked the class to count the number of stars they could see at night. The reporting of the answers the following Sunday morning varied greatly among the young kids in the children's department. Responses were given like "153" to "too many to count." Most of the children agreed that there were "bunches and bunches." That is, most except young Bobby who answered with certainty, "Three." "But, Bobby," asked the teacher, "how is it that you saw so few stars when the other children found so many?" Bobby thought a minute. Finally he answered: "Well, teacher, our backyard is awfully small."

Tragically, for many of our people, the worship vision of our own backyards is awfully small too. But it doesn't have to be. It all changed for me and my people when someone helped me to consider what was really vital in worship.

SOME EXAMPLES OF WORSHIP
IN PLANNING AND PRACTICE

I am submitting five examples of worship which took place in my last pastorate. Staff ministers of music also participated in planning and leading these worship experiences.

All of these examples occurred during Advent celebrations. Each involves laypersons (prayers, soloists, lighters of Advent candles), choral participation, symbolism (lighting of Advent candles), or responsive reading involving the congregation. Attempts were made to match sermon with musical themes. Note the worship bulletin of December 5, 1982, in which Handel's *Messiah* selections related to judgment with the sermon from Malachi and Revelation, "The Judgment of Christmas." See also the worship bulletin of November 30, 1980, with the theme of "light," including lighting of the first Advent candle, hymns about light, and the sermon topic: "Christmas Lights."

Usually there is an Advent meditation, a time for reflection, litany, or confession. One service blends the ordinance of baptism with our Lord's advent-baptism by John (who "prepared the way") into the advent celebration.

This same model of planning was used throughout the year, not merely during times of "high worship." Orders of worship follow.

First Baptist Church   Hot Springs, Arkansas

Dr. Doug Dickens   Bob Sowell, Education
Larry Bradley, Music   Phil Brown, Youth
Charlene Smith, Organist   Bernice Lowrey, Pianist

A Christian Celebration of Worship

THE MORNING WORSHIP OF GOD
DECEMBER 4, 1983
10:50 A.M.

The Organ Prelude to Worship . . . . arr. Hughes
Fantasia on "The First Nowell"

The Chiming of the Hour

MY SOUL DOTH MAGNIFY THE LORD

The Lighting of the Advent Candle

Darkness
The Choral Processional . . . . *O Come, O Come, Emmanuel*
Congregation join in singing the chorus
God's Promise and Fulfillment . . . . Micah 5:2; Luke 2:4-7
The Candle of Bethlehem . . . . Sandra Eggers
The Invocation . . . . Joe Eggers

MY SPIRIT HATH REJOICED IN GOD MY SAVIOR

An Expression of Christian Friendship
The Act of Christian Baptism

Mary Katherine Jett   Lance Porter

A Litany of Preparation

Minister: A voice cries in the wilderness: prepare a way for the
Lord.
People: Then cometh Jesus from Galilee to Jordan unto John, to
be baptized of him.
Minister: Every valley shall be lifted up, and every mountain and
hill be made low. The uneven ground shall become level,
and rough places a plain.
People: And Jesus, when he was baptized, went up straightway
out of the water: and, lo, the heavens were opened unto

him, and he saw the Spirit of God descending like a dove, and lighting upon him.

Minister: And the glory of the Lord shall be revealed, and all flesh shall see it together: for the mouth of the Lord has spoken.

People: And lo a voice from heaven, saying, This is my beloved Son in whom I am well pleased.

Hymn No. 85 ..... *O Little Town of Bethlehem* .... St. Louis

HE THAT IS MIGHTY HAS DONE
TO ME GREAT THINGS

Offertory Sentence, Offering and Meditation
Christmas Memories .... Arr. Wilson
The Reading of Holy Scripture .... Luke 1:26-56
The Pastoral Prayer
The Anthem .... *Jesus Came in Love* .... Pethel
Church Musicians Choir

HIS MERCY IS ON THEM WHO FEAR HIM

The Sermon .... Dr. Doug Dickens
THE SONG OF FAITHFUL SAINTS
Hymn No. 69 .. *O for a Thousand Tongues to Sing* .... Azmon
Concerns of the Church
The Benediction and Choral Response .... Pastor and Choir
The Organ Postlude to Worship
O Come Let Us Adore Him .... arr. Johnston

THE EVENING WORSHIP OF GOD
7:00 P.M.

The Organ Prelude to Worship
Hymn No. 82 ...... *Go Tell It on the Mountain* .... Go Tell It
Prayer and Welcome
Hymn No. 84 .... *Child in the Manger* .... Bunessan

"Welcome to the World"
written by John Lee
Presented by
The Youth Singers

Hymn No. 81 .... *O Come All Ye Faithful* ...... Adeste Fideles
Concerns of the Church
The Benediction and Organ Postlude to Worship

A Christian Celebration of Worship

THE MORNING WORSHIP OF GOD
DECEMBER 2, 1984
10:50 A.M.

The Organ Prelude to Worship .... Dexter
Behold, He Cometh
The Chiming of the Hour

BLESSED BE THE LORD GOD OF ISRAEL

The Lighting of the Advent Candle

Darkness
The Choral Processional .... *O Come, O Come, Emmanuel*
The Scripture Promise
The Candle of Prophecy .... Diane Robbins
The Invocation .... John Robbins

HE HATH VISITED AND REDEEMED HIS PEOPLE

An Expression of Christian Friendship
Hymn No. 79 .. *Come, Thou Long-Expected Jesus* ...... Hyfrydol
Prayer of Confession

God our Father, we remember that we call Him Lord who is Prince
of peace, yet our world is so plagued with war. We remember that
You so loved the world that You gave Your only begotten Son that
whosoever believes in Him should not perish, yet there are so many
in our world who are lonely and left out. We remember that the
angel announced good news of a great joy which shall come to all
people, yet many live drab, joyless lives. We remember Your promises we have failed to claim. O, God, cast out our sin, and enter in;
be born in us today. Amen.

The Pastoral Prayer
Hymn No. 83 .... *Hark! The Herald Angels Sing* .... Mendelssohn

HE HATH RAISED UP AN HORN OF SALVATION

The Offertory Prayer, Offering and Meditation

Lo, How a Rose E'er Blooming .... arr. Chatham

168

The Reading of Holy Scripture . . . . Colossians 1:24-29
The Anthem . . . . *Jesus, He Shall Be Great* . . . . Fettke
The Sermon . . . . Doug Dickens
MESSENGERS OF THE MYSTERY OF CHRISTMAS

HE SPEAKS BY THE MOUTH OF
HIS HOLY MESSENGERS

Hymn No. 82 . . . . . *Go, Tell It on the Mountain* . . . . Go Tell It
Opportunities of the Church
Benediction and Choral Response . . . . Pastor and Choir
The Organ Postlude to Worship . . . . Rand
Joy and Praise

THE EVENING WORSHIP OF GOD
7:00 P.M.

The Organ Prelude to Worship
Hymn No. 391 . . . . *Stand Up for Jesus* . . . . Webb
Prayer and Welcome
Hymn No. 327 . . . . *More About Jesus* . . . . Sweney
The Offertory Prayer, Offering, and Meditation

"Christmas Stranger"
A play by Edith Chaffee

Setting:
The living room of the Barton home

Characters:
The father, George (Joe Gross); the mother, Grace (Toni Bradley);
the children, Loralee (Gina Gilliland), Betty (Allison Davis), David
(Mike Ingram); the visitor, Jeffrey Lawrence (Eric Bremer)

The Drama Committee:
Judy Rowe, chairman; Barbara Batson, Penny Lawson,
Diane Robbins, Helen Rowe

Sound and Lighting:
Shawn Clamon, Raymond Rowe, and Mike Wiles

Special Thanks to:
Freida Gipson, and Abilities Unlimited for assistance

A Christian Celebration of Worship

THE MORNING WORSHIP OF GOD
DECEMBER 16, 1984
10:50 A.M.

JOY TO THE WORLD! THE LORD IS COME

The Handbell Prelude to Worship

O Tannenbaum; I Heard the Bells; Joy to the World .. arr. Garee

The Chiming of the Hour

The Choir Processional .... *O Come, O Come, Emmanuel*
Darkness
The Scriptural Promise
The Candle of The Shepherds .... Glee Thompson
The Invocation .... Dr. Paul Thompson

JOY TO THE EARTH! THE SAVIOR REIGNS

An Expression of Christian Friendship
Hymn No. 88 .... *Joy to the World* .... Antioch
(Stanzas 1, 2 and 3)
A Music Witness .... *Sweet Little Jesus Boy* .... Spiritual
Ruth Bremer, Soloist
Hymn No. 91 .... *The First Nowell* .... Nowell
The Offertory Prayer, Offering and Meditation

Angels We Have Heard on High .... H. Smith

NO MORE LET SINS AND SORROWS GROW

The Reading of Holy Scripture .... Matthew 2:1-12
The Pastoral Prayer
The Anthem .... *Immanuel* .... Davis/Hanvey
Adult Choir
The Sermon .... Doug Dickens
ARE YOU GOING ANYWHERE FOR CHRISTMAS?

HE RULES THE WORLD WITH TRUTH AND GRACE

Hymn No. 86 ... *It Came Upon the Midnight Clear* .... Carol
The Opportunities of the Church
Benediction .... Pastor and Congregation

> Minister: And the Word became flesh and dwelt among us, full of grace and truth; we have beheld His glory, glory as of the only Son from the Father.
> People: Joy to the world; the Lord is come: Let earth receive her
> (spoken) King; let every heart prepare Him room, and heaven and nature sing.
> Minister: Sing unto the Lord a new song; Sing unto the Lord, all the earth. Declare His glory among the nations, His marvelous works among all the people.
> People: Joy to the world; the Saviour reigns: let men their songs
> (spoken) employ; while fields and floods, rocks, hills and plains, repeat the sounding joy.
> Minister: Let the people praise You, O God; let all the people praise You. O let the nations be glad and sing for joy, for You will judge the people with equity, and govern the nations upon the earth.
> People: He rules the world with truth and grace, and makes the
> (sung) nations prove the glories of His righteousness, and wonders of His love.

The Organ Postlude to Worship .... Smith
Joy to the Wcrld

THE EVENING WORSHIP OF GOD
7:00 P.M.

The Organ Prelude to Worship
Hymn No. 87 ... *Angels From the Realms of Glory* .. Regent Square
Invocation .... Milton Raabe
An Expression of Christian Friendship
Hymn No. 89 .... *Silent Night* .... Stille Nacht
The Offertory Prayer, Offering, and Meditation

"CRADLE THE KING WITH PRAISE"
presented by the Adult Choir

Benediction
The Organ Postlude to Worship

A Christian Celebration of Worship

THE MORNING WORSHIP OF GOD
11:00 A.M.
NOVEMBER 30, 1980

The Organ Prelude to Worship .... Charlene Smith

AWAITING THE LIGHT

Darkness
A Biblical Prelude to Worship ..... Isaiah 58:8-9; 60:1-3; John 8:12
Hymn No. 76 .... *Angels from the Realms of Glory* .. Regent Square
Processional and Lighting of the Advent Candle
Church Musicians Choir and Mr. and Mrs. Lealon Worrell
The Morning Prayer .... Elgin Hamner
An Expression of Christian Fellowship
Hymn No. 68 .... *As with Gladness Men of Old* .... Dix

NEWS OF THE LIGHT

An Aspiration of Hope for the Light

Pastor: O Wisdom proceeding from the mouth of the Highest, reaching from eternity to eternity.
People: Come, teach us the way of knowledge.
Pastor: O Root of Jesse, who stands as an Ensign of the people;
People: Come and deliver us, O Lord.
Pastor: O Key of David and Scepter of Israel;
People: Come and release us from the prison of darkness and death.
Pastor: O Dayspring, splendor of eternal light and sun of righteousness:
People: Come and enlighten us, O Lord.
Pastor: O Emmanuel, our King and Lawgiver, the expectation and Savior of the nations:
People: Come and save us, O Lord.

Hymn No. 88 .... Light of the World
The Light of the World Is Jesus
The Offertory Prayer and Morning Offering

172

THE LIGHT REVEALED

The Reading of Holy Scripture .... John 1:1-14
The Pastoral Prayer
The Choral Worship .. *God So Loved the World* .... Stainer
Church Musicians Choir
The Sermon .... CHRISTMAS LIGHTS ...... Doug Dickens

LET YOUR LIGHT SO SHINE

Hymn No. 457 .... *Send the Light* .... McCabe
Concerns of the Church
The Benediction and Choral Response
The Organ Postlude to Worship

THE EVENING WORSHIP OF GOD
7:00 P.M.

The Organ Prelude to Worship .... Charlene Smith
Hymn No. 345 .... *Beneath the Cross of Jesus* ... St. Christopher
The Evening Prayer .... Clyde Felts
Hymn No. 443 .. *In Christ There Is No East or West* ...... St. Peter
An Expression of Christian Fellowship
Hymn No. 459 .... *Ye Christian Heralds!* .... Duke Street
The Offertory Prayer and Evening Offering
Choral Music .... Mini-concert by the Youth Singers
The Sermon .... Doug Dickens
GIVE THANKS FOR WHAT? (Psalm 103)
Hymn No. 440 .... *Hark, the Voice of Jesus Calling*
Concerns of the Church .... Elleside
The Benediction
The Organ Postlude to Worship

A Christian Celebration of Worship

THE MORNING WORSHIP OF GOD
DECEMBER 5, 1982
10:50 A.M.

The Organ Prelude to Worship . . . . Wilson
Christmas Memories

COME, THOU LONG-EXPECTED JESUS

The Chiming of the Hour
The Lighting of the Advent Candle

Darkness
Choral Procession . . . . *O Come, O Come, Emmanuel*
Promise and Fulfillment . . . . Micah 5:2; Luke 2:4-7
The Candle of Bethlehem . . . . Barbara Larkin
The Invocation . . . . Jim Larkin

HOPE OF ALL THE WORLD THOU ART

An Expression of Christian Friendship
Hymn No. 79 . . *Come, Thou Long-Expected Jesus* . . . . . . Hyfrydol
An Advent Meditation

God our Father, we remember that we call Him Lord who is Prince of peace, yet our world is so plagued with war. We remember that You so loved the world that You gave Your only begotten Son that whosoever believes in Him should not perish, yet there are so many in our world who are lonely and left out. We remember that the angel announced good news of a great joy which shall come to all people, yet many live drab, joyless lives. We remember Your promises we have failed to claim. O God, cast out our sin, and enter in; be born in us today, Amen.

Hymn No. 83 . . . . *Hark! The Herald Angels Sing* . . . . Mendelssohn
The Offertory Prayer, Offering and Meditation

Infant Holy, Infant Lowly . . . . Arr. Kerri

174

FROM OUR FEARS AND SINS RELEASE US

The Reading of Holy Scripture ..... Malachi 2:10; 4:6; Rev. 22:7-13
The Music of Advent .... Handel's *Messiah*

Thus Saith the Lord .... Dr. Paul Hammond
But who may abide the day of His coming? ... Dr. Paul Hammond
And He Shall Purify .... Church Musicians Choir

The Pastoral Prayer
The Sermon .... Dr. Doug Dickens
THE JUDGMENT OF CHRISTMAS

JOY OF EVERY LONGING HEART

Hymn No. 90 .... *Good Christian Men, Rejoice* ... In Dulci Jubilo
Concerns of the Church
The Benediction and Response .... Pastor and Choir
The Organ Postlude to Worship

O Come, Let Us Adore Him .... Arr. Johnston

THE EVENING WORSHIP OF GOD
7:00 P.M.

The Organ Prelude to Worship
Hymn No. 82 ..... *Go, Tell It on the Mountain* .... Go Tell It
The Invocation .... Jim J.
An Expression of Christian Friendship
Hymn No. 89 ...... *Silent Night, Holy Night* .... Stille Nacht
Mary's Song .... Miriam Woosley, Soloist
Hymn No. 80 .... *Away in a Manger* .... Mueller
The Offertory Prayer, Offering, and Meditation
He Shall Be Great .... The Youth Singers
The Sermon .... MEN AND MISSIONS .... Dr. Carl Overton
(Acts 13:1-3)
Hymn No. 88 .... *Joy to the World!* .... Antioch
Concerns of the Church
The Benediction and Organ Postlude to Worship

If you know of anyone having difficulty hearing during our Worship Service, please contact an usher. Small hearing devices are available for your use.

HARDY CLEMONS
Lubbock, Texas

[Worship is a priority at Hardy Clemon's church. His church's promotional materials make that clear. An excerpt from their promotional materials follows.]

Worship at Second Baptist Church is primary; it is here the congregation finds meaning for its task. Worship reaches its highest point as we gather in the worship center each Sunday, then continues throughout the week as we live out the worthship of God in touching the lives of others.

Worship each week is built around a theme which is developed through music, prayer, Scripture, the proclaimed word, and commitment of life. Laypersons and the pastors share leadership in worship.

Worship includes seasonal emphases, as may be seen, in the observances of Advent and Holy Week. During the weeks immediately preceding Christmas, the congregation is reminded of the personal preparation necessary for the Christ event to be meaningful. Holy Week also provides a time of personal introspection as the events leading to and including the crucifixion are reexperienced. Resurrection Sunday then ushers the worshiping congregation into the joyful Eastertide season. Two other seasons of joy that are celebrated are Epiphany and Pentecost.

Worship at Second Baptist can be formal or informal, musical or spoken, silent or verbalized; but always it is the act of discovering God's worth plus the commitment to serve Him by expressing that worth to a world that hungers for true value.

[Clemons described how he and his staff prepare for Sunday. A distinctive of his worship planning is his heavy use of the lectionary.]

Our approach to putting Sunday morning worship together is as follows: We use the common lectionary unless there is some specific reason to set it aside and choose another passage of Scripture which will serve as the basis for worship on the coming Sunday. I select a sermon title and suggest a specific focus of one or more Scripture passages to our worship coordinator who is Robert Moore. Robert and our music staff put together suggestions for the order of worship—choosing hymns, special music of various types, etc.

The worship staff brings a rough draft to the pastoral staff on Tuesday afternoon, and we seek to finalize the worship plan for the coming Sunday morning. We use the passages from the lectionary as the basis for our Wednesday evening Bible study around the supper tables. We also check the lectionary for passages which might be appropriate for funeral worship and/or wedding worship which may occur during a particular week's activity.

Our basic theology of worship is that worship should be spelled "worthship." Our attempt is to give people an experience of worth that gets them in touch with the God who is the Source and Creator of worth in our world. We want worship to call people "from this vain world's golden store" to focus on the reality of who God is as Creator, Redeemer, and Friend. We want worship to include the elements of praise, meditation, proclamation, and commitment. We particularly feel that worship should conclude with a commitment on every person's part to go back into his or her daily life on the basis of new worth that has been discovered in the midst of worship on that particular day. The announcement time is a time of "opportunities for response" for people to make in equipping themselves for ministry or engaging in actual ministry, and in that light we see the announcements as a vital part of the worship experience.

The Worship of God

First Sunday in Advent—December 1, 1985
8:30 and 10:45 A.M.

We gladly welcome visitors today! Brochures about Second Baptist are available near the north entrance.

Organ Music .... Norman Goad, organist
O Come, O Come, Immanuel .... Paul Manz
Call to Worship .... Robert Moore
Hymn 303 .... *Thou Whose Almighty Word*
Tune: Italian Hymn
Affirmation of Faith (in the Words of St. John)

> We believe that God is Spirit, and they that worship Him must worship Him in spirit and in truth.
> We believe that God is Light, and that if we walk in the light, as He is in the light, we have fellowship one with another.
> We believe that Jesus Christ is the Son of God, and that God has given to us eternal life, and this life is in His Son.
> We believe that He is the Resurrection and the Life, and that those who believe in Him, though they were dead, yet shall they live.
> We believe that we are children of God, and that He has given us of His Spirit.
> We believe that if we confess our sins, He is faithful and just to forgive us our sins, and to cleanse us from all uncleanness.
> We believe that the world passes away and the desire to possess it, but He that does the will of God abides forever. Amen.

Welcome / Concerns of the Congregation
Silence / Prayer of Intercession .... Penny Vann, 8:30
Bill Kingsberry, 10:45
10:45 Children's Time
10:45 Choral Witness .. *Come, O Jesus* .... Garry Cornell
Old Testament Reading .... Joy Vann, 8:30
Jeremiah 33:14-16, RSV .... Anne Letalien, 10:45

"Behold, the days are coming, says the LORD when I will fulfil the promise I made to the house of Israel and the house of Judah. In those days and at that time I will cause a righteous Branch to spring forth for David; and he shall execute justice and righteousness in the land. In those days Judah will be saved and Jerusalem will dwell securely. And this is the name by which it will be called: 'The Lord is our righteousness.'"

Vocal Witness ... *Lo, How a Rose E'er Blooming* ...... Praetorius
Becky Finley, soprano

Lighting of the First Advent Candle
Judie and Jared Darnell, 8:30
Charles, Donna, Traci and Troy Scarborough, 10:45

Hymn 78 .... *O Come, O Come, Immanuel*

Sermon .... Hardy Clemons
GOD'S PROMISE FOR CHRISTMAS

Commitment Hymn 140 .... *O Word of God Incarnate*
Tune: Passion Chorale
(Persons wishing to unite with this congregation
may come forward during this hymn.)

Offertory Sentences

Tithes and Offerings

Musical Offering .... Stephen Finley, pianist

Announcements

Recognition of Persons Seeking Membership

Dismissal

Choral Departing Song .... *Angels We Have Heard*

Angels we have heard on high, Sweetly singing o'er the plains:
And the mountains in reply, Echoing their joyous strains.
Gloria in excelsis Deo! Gloria in excelsis Deo!

No SUNDAY NIGHT AT 7

The Worship of God

On the Lord's Day—June 22, 1986
8:30 and 10:45 A.M.

We gladly welcome visitors today! Brochures about Second Baptist Church are available near the north entrance.

Music for Worship .... Norman Goad
Prelude and Fugue in F-Major .... J. S. Bach
Anthem .... *Cast Thy Burden Upon the Lord*
Call to Worship .... Psalm 43 (RSV) .... Robert Moore

>Leader: Vindicate me, O God, and defend my cause against an un-godly people; from deceitful and unjust men deliver me!
>People: For thou art the God in whom I take refuge; why hast thou cast me off?
>Leader: Why go I mourning because of the oppression of the enemy?
>People: O send out thy light and thy truth; let them lead me, let them bring me to thy holy hill and to thy dwelling!
>Leader: Then I will go to the altar of God, to God my exceeding joy;
>People: and I will praise thee with the lyre, O God, my God.
>Leader: Why are you cast down, O my soul, and why are you disquieted within me?
>All: Hope in God; for I shall again praise him, my help and my God.

Hymn of Courage 37 .... *A Mighty Fortress Is Our God*
The Reading of the Epistle .... Hardy Clemons
Galatians 3:23-29 (GNB)

>But before the time for faith came, the Law kept us all locked up as prisoners until this coming faith should be revealed. And so the Law was in charge of us until Christ came, in order that we might then be put right with God through faith. Now that the time for faith is here, the Law is no longer in charge of us.
>It is through faith that all of you are God's sons in union with Christ Jesus. You were baptized into union with Christ, and now you are clothed, so to speak, with the life of Christ himself. So there is no difference between Jews and Gentiles, between slaves and free men, between men and women; you are all one in union with Christ Jesus. If you belong to Christ, then you are the descendants of Abraham and will receive what God has promised.

The Pharisee and the Publican ...... Heinrich Schuetz (1585-1672)
Vocal Quartet and the Liturgical Dancers

Welcome / Concerns of the Congregation
Prayer of Intercession . . . . Rod McClendon, 8:30
Frank Imke, 10:45
10:45 Children's Time . . . . Nancy Campbell
Hymn 339 . . . . *It Is Well with My Soul*
Old Testament Reading . . . . Madeline Douglas, 8:30
1 Kings 19:9-14 (GNB) . . . . Anita Bass, 10:45

> There he went into a cave to spend the night.
> Suddenly the Lord spoke to him, "Elijah, what are you doing here?"
> He answered, "Lord God Almighty, I have always served you—you alone. But the people of Israel have broken their covenant with you, torn down your altars, and killed all your prophets. I am the only one left—and they are trying to kill me!"
> "Go out and stand before me on top of the mountain," the Lord said to him. Then the Lord passed by and sent a furious wind that split the hills and shattered the rocks—but the Lord was not in the wind. The wind stopped blowing, and then there was an earthquake—but the Lord was not in the earthquake. After the earthquake there was a fire—but the Lord was not in the fire. And after the fire there was the soft whisper of a voice.
> When Elijah heard it, he covered his face with his cloak and went out and stood at the entrance of the cave. A voice said to him, "Elijah, what are you doing here?"
> He answered, "Lord God Almighty, I have always served you—you alone. But the people of Israel have broken their covenant with you, torn down your altars, and killed all your prophets. I am the only one left—and they are trying to kill me."

Offertory Sentences
Tithes and Offerings
Musical Offering . . . . Conley Cook, baritone
It Is Enough from *Elijah* . . . . Mendelssohn
Sermon . . . . Hardy Clemons
MEETING GOD IN SURPRISING PLACES
Sounds of Silence . . . . Ronda Stewart, flutist
Commitment Hymn . . . . (insert)
Dear Lord and Father of Us All
(Persons wishing to unite with this congregation
are invited to come forward during this hymn.)
Announcements / Recognition of Persons Seeking Membership
Celebrating the Ordination of Nancy Campbell . . . . Carlos Byrd
Dismissal
Departing Song . . . . . *It Is Well with My Soul* . . . . (chorus)
Postlude

WILLIAM E. HULL
Shreveport, Louisiana

[William Hull has developed a workable and pragmatic system for long-range planning. He plans worship four times a year. Of special interest are his efforts at worship evaluation. A brief explanation of his planning process, a congregational questionnaire created for evaluating worship, and two orders of worship follow.]

The pastor and minister of music are the primary planning agents for worship in our church. I like a carefully integrated service to give cumulative force to the theme being emphasized. We strive to have the call to worship, hymns, anthem, Scripture reading, sermon, and other features all reinforce a common purpose.

To accomplish this, I plan worship four times a year: from New Years to Easter, from Easter to commencement, from commencement to Labor Day, and from Labor Day to Christmas. I try to give the minister of music the basic themes of each service two or three months in advance. On that basis he orders music and begins to collect suitable materials for the order of service. Approximately one week in advance, he drafts a tentative order of service which I review and revise with him. We then share this with our entire ministerial staff so that all may have input in light of program assignments. Following Sunday, we review the service as to sequence, timing, effectiveness for television, and feedback from the congregation. Periodically, I ask a group in our church to evaluate worship and have, at times, used a questionnaire to seek the views of the entire congregation.

Baptism liberates from death. The old self must die and be buried, and a new self must be raised up. Each day we must learn to die, to let go, to be plunged under the waters so that God might pull us forth like newborn babies. Baptism is a dress rehearsal for death. We must die many deaths, and we must be born again of "water and the spirit"—and again and again. Baptism is the once-and-for-all, continuing experience of death and rebirth, repentance and conversion.

William H. Willimon

O HAPPY DAY THAT FIXED MY CHOICE

Prelude: Medley of Baptismal Hymns .... Sherry L. Upshaw

Expressions of Fellowship and Registration of Guests   William E. Hull

A Call to Celebration .... Sanctuary Choir

O Happy Day That Fixed My Choice .... Happy Day

WELL MAY THIS GLOWING HEART REJOICE

A Prayer of Rejoicing .... Gregory L. Hunt

Hymn of Praise .... Number 164

O Thou God of My Salvation .... Regent Square

Responsive Reading .... Gregory D. Bunch and Congregation

"Meaning of Baptism" .... Number 38

HE TAUGHT ME HOW TO WATCH AND PRAY

A Call to the Children .... Sanctuary Choir

O Happy Day That Fixed My Choice .... Happy Day

Children's Sermon: Seven Ducks in Muddy Water .. William E. Hull

Hymn of Commitment .... Number 386

O Jesus, I Have Promised .... Angel's Story

Prayer of Thanksgiving .... Katye Lee Posey

The Offertory .... Sherry L. Upshaw

O Love That Wilt Not Let Me Go .... arr. Alice Jordan

AND LIVE REJOICING EVERY DAY

Choral Music .... Sanctuary Choir

O Thou Who in Jordan .... St. Michel's

Baptismal Homily .... William E. Hull

THE WITNESS OF WATER (1 John 5:6-8)

HAPPY DAY! HAPPY DAY!

An Affirmation of Baptism

Pastor: We come in sign and symbol.
People: **The water is a sign, and the act of baptism is a symbol.**
Pastor: We come in belief and obedience.
People: **Our belief is in Christ, and our obedience is to his command.**
Pastor: We come to observe and remember.
People: **In observing the baptism of these, we remember our own vows.**

Baptism as Confirmation of a Childhood Faith

Brooks Edward Byrd   Karen Elizabeth Covington
Jami Kendall Elrod   Rebecca Ashton Fox
Bobby Ross Lewis

Baptism as Conversion to New Life in Christ . . . . Sukalyan Saha
Baptism as Consecration
in a New Heritage of Faith . . . . William Sherwood Bailey, Jr.

WHEN JESUS WASHED MY SINS AWAY

Hymn of Decision . . . . Number 385

Come, Holy Spirit, Dove Divine . . . . Maryton

Presentation of New Members . . . . Gregory L. Hunt
A Baptismal Benediction . . . . William E. Hull
The Response of the People . . . . Solo and Congregation

O Happy Day That Fixed My Choice . . . . Happy Day

Happy day, happy day, When Jesus washed my sins away!
He taught me how to watch and pray, And live rejoicing every day;
Happy day, Happy day, When Jesus washed my sins away! Amen.

Closing Voluntary . . . . Sherry L. Upshaw

Holy God, We Praise Thy Name . . . . arr. Paul Manz

The Pastor's messages are made available to members and friends through the Shreveport Sermon Ministry. A selection of sermons is edited in printed form and every message is reproduced on standard cassette tape. For further information contact any of the church offices.

"The only ultimate way to conquer evil is to let it be smothered within a willing, living human being. When it is absorbed there, like blood in a sponge or a spear thrown into one's heart, it loses its power and goes no further."

Gale D. Webbe, *The Night and Nothing*

WE ASSEMBLE IN GOD'S NAME

Opening Voluntary .... Sherry L. Upshaw

Rhosymedre .... Ralph Vaughan Williams

Expressions of Fellowship .... Gregory L. Hunt
Call to Worship .... Sanctuary Choir

Come We That Love the Lord .... C. L. Bass

Song of Fellowship .... Duke Street
O Lord Who Hast This Table Spread
Invocation .... Gregory D. Bunch

TO PRAISE GOD'S FAITHFULNESS

Organ Meditation .... Sherry L. Upshaw
Anthem .... Sanctuary Choir

For All the Saints .... R. Vaughan Williams

In Memoriam ..... Our Beloved Dead, 1985-86 ... William E. Hull
Hymn .... Number 471

There's a Land That Is Fairer than Day ...... Sweet By and By

A Prayer of Remembrance .... Bitsy Smith
Offertory .... Sherry L. Upshaw

The Saints' Delight .... arr. Dale Wood

TO PROCLAIM GOD'S WORD

Solo .... Donna Dugas, Soprano

The Twenty-Third Psalm .... Albert Mallotte

Communion Meditation .... William E. Hull
Bitburg Revisited

186

CELEBRATE THE LORD'S SUPPER

Hymn . . . . Number 392

Here at Thy Table, Lord . . . . Bread of Life

A Prayer for the Communion of Saints . . . . William E. Hull
The Words of Institution and Invitation . . . . William E. Hull
The Sharing of the Bread . . . . Gregory L. Hunt
Choral Meditation . . . . Sanctuary Choir

O Sacred Head . . . . J. S. Bach

The Sharing of the Cup . . . . William E. Hull
Choral Meditation . . . . Sanctuary Choir

I Come With Joy to Meet My Lord . . . . Land of Rest

TO RESPOND IN FAITH

Hymn of Decision . . . . Number 380

The Church's One Foundation . . . . Aurelia

Presentation of New Members . . . . William E. Hull
Choral Benediction . . . . Sanctuary Choir

Ascription of Praise . . . . David Schwoebel

Closing Voluntary . . . . Sherry L. Upshaw

When I Can Read My Title Clear . . . . arr. Dale Wood

IN MEMORIAM
May 22, 1985—May 25, 1986

Mrs. E. J. (Pearl) Adams	Mrs. Lessie B. Davis	Harold Calvert Jones
Edwin P. Alexander	Arvol Ellard	William R. Lusby
Ralph H. Allor	Clarence William Evans	Mrs. Herbert (Irma) Mayer
Robert D. Anderson	E. Ulmer Fogle	Mrs. Ralph (Lucille)
Mrs. F. V. (Evelyn) Atkins	Mrs. Wesley C. (Margaret)	McMahon
Thurston E. Baggett	Ford, Jr.	Thomas Robert Moffett
Mrs. C. S. (Aleen) Barr	W. A. Fortson	Sidney Doyle Nicklas
Charles F. (Rick) Biggs, Jr.	Mrs. W. A. (Julia) Fortson	Miss Marilyn D. Prather
Mrs. Bussey Todd Boone	Dewey O'Neal Furr, Jr.	James Malcolm Robinson, Jr.
Mrs. Mattie Lou Braswell	Mrs. Joseph E. (Frances	Miss Gertrude Sims
Mrs. J. M. (Lillian)	"Mac") Heard	J. C. Smith
Browning	Robert Smith Hendrick,	Paschal K. Smith
Mrs. Eunice Buckhalt	Sr.	Andrian Roscoe Snider
Mrs. Harold (Dollie)	Miss Lorraine Herndon	Miss Gertrude Taylor
Campbell	Mrs. R. M. (Nell) Jemison	Mrs. J. M. (Norma) Tinsley
Brock E. Collins	Miss Lynn Jennings	Ralph Trussell

QUESTIONNAIRE ON WORSHIP AND PREACHING
Congregational Survey—Part I

(In the *Church Chimes* of March 7, 1981, our Pastor explained how we might secure greater input from the laity in designing services of worship. This strategy includes a poll to determine how members and other participants now view what we are doing and too identify areas in which they would like to consider possible changes. Please ponder the following inquiries and give us your response to every question either by turning in this *Chimes* or by completing a duplicate form which will be available to every youth and adult in both the Sunday School and worship services on Sunday.)

1. At present we provide a printed order of service at each major worship event. In your opinion, these guides are (choose one):
   ( ) Important and should be provided regularly
   ( ) Optional and should be provided only on special occasions
   ( ) Unimportant and should not be provided
2. Typically, we have included the following elements in most Sunday morning services of worship. Please rate the importance of each as a regular part of worship:

ELEMENT OF WORSHIP	IMPORTANT— use regularly	OPTIONAL— use occasionally	UNIMPORTANT— use seldom or none
(1) Organ Prelude			
(2) Processional by worship leaders			
(3) Choral call to worship			
(4) Invocation			
(5) Welcome and Registration of Guests			
(6) Anthem by the choir			
(7) Pastoral prayer			
(8) Chidren's Sermons			
(9) Doxology			
(10) Offertory Prayer			
(11) Offering with organ offertory			
(12) Scripture Reading			
(13) Solo, Duet, or other Special Music			
(14) Sermon			
(15) Invitation to church membership			
(16) Presentation of new members			
(17) Opportunities for Service			
(18) Benediction			
(19) Choral response to benediction			
(20) Organ Postlude			

3. In each service we use at least one lay worship leader in a variety of assign-ments (e.g. prayer, Scripture reading, welcome). How do you rate the impor-tance of this participation?
   ( ) Important—use laypersons regularly
   ( ) Optional—use laypersons occasionally
   ( ) Unimportant—use laypersons seldom or none
4. At present our morning services are scheduled to begin at 10:45, to con-clude at 12:00, hence to last one hour and fifteen minutes.
   Your preferences:

To begin:	To end:	To last:
( ) 10:30	( ) 11:30	( ) 45 minutes
( ) 10:45	( ) 11:45	( ) 1 hour
( ) 11:00	( ) 12:00	( ) 1 hr. & 15 min.
( ) Other _____	( ) Other _____	( ) Other _____

5 Throughout the year, a number of special emphases are featured in the Sunday morning worship service. Please evaluate the significance of each.

SPECIAL WORSHIP EMPHASES	IMPORTANT—observe annually	OPTIONAL—not observe every year	UNIMPORTANT—do not observe
(1) Leadership Dedication Day— Ordination of deacons _____			
(2) Church Heritage Day— Anniversary Sunday _____			
(3) Youth Week Sunday _____			
(4) Stewardship Sundays (2 or 3) Annual budget promotion _____			
(5) Holy Week: Palm Sunday and Easter Sunday (2) _____			
(6) FBC School Baccalaureate Service Recognition of High School Seniors _____			
(7) Memorial Day Sunday honoring of beloved dead _____			
(8) Parent-Child Dedication Service 2 Sundays (June and December) _____			
(9) Independence Day Sunday patriotic emphasis near July 4 _____			
(10) Fifty Year Fellowship Sunday recognition of long-term members _____			
(11) Pastor's Anniversary Sunday _____			
(12) World Mission Sundays (2 or 3) Parade of Flags, Mission Blitz Team _____			
(13) Advent—Christmas services (3 or 4) _____			
(14) Student Day at Christmas service use of college and seminary students			

6. In conclusion, listed below are a number of general characteristics which can be applied to the "style" in which worship is conducted. Based on your understanding of these terms, indicate the direction in which you would like to see our services move in the future.

WORSHIP CHARACTERISTICS	More of this characteristic	About the same as at present	Less of this characteristic
(1) Formality—dignity _____			
(2) Spontaneity—extemporaneousness _____			
(3) Reverence—holiness _____			
(4) Congregational participation— lay involvement _____			
(5) Liturgy—planned aids _____			
(6) Drama—pageantry _____			
(7) Innovation—experimentation _____			
(8) Humor—laughter			

QUESTIONNAIRE ON WORSHIP AND PREACHING
Congregational Survey—Part II

1. Regarding outside lighting, our shutters may be set in three positions. Which do you prefer for regular morning services?
   - ☐ Shutters entirely closed, blocking outside light, sanctuary illumined entirely by inside light.
   - ☐ Shutters half open, admitting outside light indirectly to supplement inside light.
   - ☐ Shutters fully open, admitting outside light directly to provide primary illumination of the sanctuary.
2. Regarding inside lighting, our equipment permits a wide variety of settings in different parts of the sanctuary (e.g., pew area, pulpit area, choir area). Which of the following approaches corresponds most closely to your personal preference?
   - ☐ Illumine the entire sanctuary evenly and leave that setting throughout the service.
   - ☐ Illumine the pew areas evenly for worshipers throughout the service but turn up the pulpit area lights to focus on preacher or choir or other worship leaders during their presentations.
   - ☐ Vary not only pulpit area settings as just described, but also raise or lower pew area lighting as appropriate (e.g., brighten lights during hymns, dim lights during prayers).
3. Current practice is for latecomers to be seated at specified times in the service during hymns and organ interludes. Which one of the following best describes your desires?
   - ☐ Continue present practice unchanged.
   - ☐ Provide special section in the rear where latecomers may be seated whenever they arrive.
   - ☐ Allow latecomers to seat themselves wherever they please whenever they arrive.
4. Current practice is for a number of worshipers to leave the morning service early, usually during the invitation hymn. Which one of the following best describes your desires?
   - ☐ Continue present practice unchanged.
   - ☐ Provide a special section for those leaving early so as to minimize the distraction for those who remain.
   - ☐ Discourage the present practice by adopting a church policy requesting all worshipers to remain until the postlude begins.
5. At present we typically sing three congregational hymns in the morning worship service (opening, offertory, invitation). In your opinion, this is:
   - ☐ Too many   ☐ Too few   ☐ About right
6. There are a number of musical "styles" for congregational singing. Based on your understanding of these types, indicate the direction in which you would like to see our services move in the future (answer each part).

TYPES OF
CONGREGATIONAL SINGING

	More of this type music	About the same as at present	Less of this type music
(1) Traditional hymns that are widely recognized to have a quality tune and text	☐	☐	☐
(2) Gospel songs largely out of the revivalist tradition that primarily express one's personal testimony	☐	☐	☐
(3) Contemporary songs whose texts address current issues and whose tunes reflect more recent musical styles	☐	☐	☐
(4) Brief choruses, usually learned and sung by memory, that typically stand in the tradition of religious folk singing	☐	☐	☐

7. There are some 500 selections for congregational singing in the *Baptist Hymnal* used in our sanctuary at present. Based on your evaluation of this collection, how many of these selections would you like for us to sing on a regular basis?
   ☐ 125 or less (under 25%)
   ☐ 125 to 250 (25% to 50%)
   ☐ 250 to 375 (50% to 75%)
   ☐ 375 or more (over 75%)
8. Present practice is to stand for most congregational singing. Your preference:
   ☐ Stand for most congregational singing.
   ☐ Stand and sit about equally for congregational singing.
   ☐ Sit for most congregational singing.
9. At present, the organ is the only instrument that normally accompanies congregational singing in the Sunday morning services. Which one of the following do you think would be most effective as a regular practice?
   ☐ Continue to use organ only.
   ☐ Regularly use both organ and piano accompaniment.
   ☐ Use both organ and piano plus other orchestra instruments as available.
10. Currently it is typical to have two special musical presentations in the Sunday morning service, an anthem by the Sanctuary Choir, and a solo by selected individuals. As you see it:
    ☐ This is about the right number and balance of special musical presentations.
    ☐ This is too much special music; have an anthem or solo but not both.
    ☐ This is too little special music; have even greater variety by using other choirs and by having more ensemble groups to sing.
11. Many worshipers tend to view special music as falling into two broad categories: (a) "Classical," by which they mean the kind of music, whether traditional or contemporary, that appeals to those with a cultivated appreciation of musical excellence; (b) "Popular," by which they mean the kind of

music that appeals to those with or without an acquired taste for serious music primarily because of its emotional impact upon the hearer. Within the context of these categories, what "mix" would you like in our Sunday morning worship services?

☐ Mainly "classical" special music, with the more "popular" type reserved for Sunday evening and special occasions such as revivals.

☐ Mainly "popular" special music, with the more "classical" type reserved for special occasions such as choir concerts.

☐ A mixture of "classical" and "popular" special music that favors the "classical."

☐ A mixture of "classical" and "popular" special music that favors the "popular."

☐ A deliberate balance between "classical" and "popular" that gives each of them equal weight.

12. Recently our Pastor used a series of *Chimes* columns to explain his approach to "preaching by objectives." Analyzing the first five years of Sunday morning sermons, he reported the following weight given to each major purpose of our church. Please evaluate the adequacy of this ratio in each category:

SERMON CATEGORY	Too much—preach less	Present ratio about right	Too little—preach more
(1) Worship—13.6% Strengthening our relation to God	☐	☐	☐
(2) Outreach—19.7% Winning others to Christ	☐	☐	☐
(3) Nurture—25.8% Growing in Christian discipleship	☐	☐	☐
(4) Pastoral Care—16.9% Strengthening and encouraging one another	☐	☐	☐
(5) Mission Service—14.6% Serving the needy at home and abroad	☐	☐	☐
(6) Administration—9.4% Mobilizing resources to accomplish our mission	☐	☐	☐

13. In a typical service, presenting the sermon averages 23-27 minutes and extending the invitation averages 2-3 minutes, for a total average of 25-30 minutes for both. How much time do you think should be devoted to the sermon and invitation?

☐ 20 minutes or less
☐ 20 to 25 minutes
☐ 25 to 30 minutes
☐ 30 minutes or more

14. Sermons have many elements of strength or weakness that determine their overall effectiveness. Taking our Pastor's morning preaching as a whole, carefully rate its effectiveness in the following areas:

193

CRITERIA

	Excellent	Good	Average	Poor	Failure
(1) The sermons are soundly rooted in Scripture	☐	☐	☐	☐	☐
(2) The sermons spring not only from Scripture but from the personal experience of the preacher	☐	☐	☐	☐	☐
(3) The sermons show thorough preparation and careful thought	☐	☐	☐	☐	☐
(4) The sermons are clearly organized and move to a logical climax	☐	☐	☐	☐	☐
(5) The sermons are interesting and well-illustrated	☐	☐	☐	☐	☐
(6) The sermons strengthen the relation between pastor and people	☐	☐	☐	☐	☐
(7) The sermons address a broad spectrum of human needs	☐	☐	☐	☐	☐
(8) The sermons appeal to a wide spectrum of ages and backgrounds	☐	☐	☐	☐	☐
(9) The sermons are relevant to current events, community needs, and seasonal emphases	☐	☐	☐	☐	☐
(10) The sermons call the lost to new life in Christ	☐	☐	☐	☐	☐
(11) The sermons convey an urgency that demands decision and response	☐	☐	☐	☐	☐
(12) The sermons sound a prophetic note that convicts of sin	☐	☐	☐	☐	☐
(13) The sermons inspire and motivate the hearer to deeper dedication	☐	☐	☐	☐	☐
(14) The sermons explain the basic beliefs and practices of our faith	☐	☐	☐	☐	☐
(15) The sermons provide practical guidance for daily living	☐	☐	☐	☐	☐

15. At present, we baptize on Sunday morning near beginning of the service. Your preference:
    ☐ Sunday morning near the beginning of service
    ☐ Sunday morning near end of service
    ☐ Sunday evening service
    ☐ Some other time (i.e. in special service)

16. At present, we celebrate the Lord's Supper six times per year. In your judgment this is:
    ☐ Too often—observe less frequently
    ☐ Too seldom—observe more frequently
    ☐ About right—continue present frequency

Thank you for completing this questionnaire. To aid us in evaluating responses, please identify yourself as follows:

STATUS
( ) FBC church member
( ) FBC Sunday School member
( ) FBC visitor or prospect
( ) Other

AGE
( ) Youth (13-18)
( ) Young Adult (18-35)
( ) Median Adult (35-60)
( ) Adult (60-over)

LENGTH IN FBC
( ) 5 years or less
( ) 5-25 years
( ) 25-50 years
( ) 50 years or more

SEX
( ) Male
( ) Female

WORSHIP PARTICIPATION
( ) Regular (75%-over)
( ) Irregular (25-75%)
( ) Very seldom (25%-under)
( ) Unable to attend
(e.g. homebound, work)

KEN LISTER
Greenville, South Carolina

[Ken is a minister of music. He does a quality job of planning creative and meaningful worship services. The key factor in Ken's worship planning is developing a central theme. The entire worship service revolves around the theme of the day. A few remarks concerning his planning process and several of his orders of worship follow.]

Our worship planning process begins with the pastor's projecting sermon themes, titles, and Scriptures for at least a three-month period. I take these topics and Scriptures, share them with the organist and pianist, and begin to plan our services using the central theme of the sermon. The hymns, anthems, other special music such as solos, and the instrumental music will relate to the central theme as much as possible. I particularly try to tie the anthem and the invitation hymn closely to the central theme. After I finish with the worship plan, the pastor reviews it for any further refinement or for any changes that might need to be made. Our congregation has expressed appreciation for the way our services relate and are woven together.

We are continually fine tuning our worship planning at weekly staff meetings and in conversations about worship. Communication is important in good worship planning as is planning ahead.

The Worship of God
Sunday, November 2, 1986

MORNING WORSHIP   10:55 A.M.

Broadcast over WMRB—1490 on the Dial

Prelude .... *Prelude and Fugue in A-minor* ...... J. S. Bach
Concerns of the Church
Preparation for Worship
Meditation .... *Fairest Lord Jesus* .... David Johnson

WORSHIP THROUGH PRAISE

Chiming of the Hour
Call to Worship
Now Let Every Tongue Adore Thee .... J. S. Bach
Invocation and Lord's Prayer .... Bill Penick
Hymn of Praise No. 11
Praise the Lord! Ye Heavens Adore Him .... Hyfrydol
Ministry of Hospitality

WORSHIP IN STEWARDSHIP

The Morning Offering
Hymn of Stewardship No. 262 .... Euclid
Make Me a Blessing
Offertory Prayer .... Jon Rainbow
Offertory .... *Andante (Sonata No. 2)* .... Rheinberger
Doxology .... Old 100th
Praise God, from Whom All Blessings Flow

Praise God, from whom all blessings flow;
Praise him, all creatures here below;
Praise him above, ye heav'nly host;
Praise Father, Son, and Holy Ghost.

198

WORSHIP IN HIS WORD

Scripture . . . . Luke 14:12-24 . . . . Pat Bailey
Invitation to Prayer
Pastoral Prayer . . . . Raymond Bailey
Anthem . . . . *Seek the Lord* . . . . Anna Laura Page

Instrumental Ensemble:
Jan Ford, Ginger Putnam, Beth O'Rear, Ginny Williams—Strings
Gela Hendrix, Kim Smith—Flute
Handbell Choir—Rick Kalk, Director

Meditation . . . . FEASTIVAL . . . . Raymond Bailey
Responsive Reading No. 569
Observance of the Lord's Supper

WORSHIP IN HIS SERVICE

Hymn of Commitment No. 414 . . . . Seminary
Because I Have Been Given Much
World Hunger Offering
Benediction
Choral Benediction . . . . *Prayer for Blessing* . . . . . David Schwoebel
Postlude . . . . *Allegro (Sonata No. 6)* . . . . Rheinberger

---

The Sanctuary flowers are in memory of Richard M. Rice by Mrs. Richard M. Rice.

SUNDAY EVENING SCHEDULE

5:00 p.m.—Seminars by Jon Rainbow and Pat Bailey
Youth Choir Rehearsal
6:00 p.m.—Worship—Jon Rainbow
Music—Young Adult Choir
7:00 p.m.—DiscipleLife
Sanctuary Choir Rehearsal

The Worship of God

MORNING WORSHIP   Sunday, March 30, 1986   10:55 A.M.
Broadcast over WMRB—1490 on the Dial

Organ Prelude .... *Intrada* .... G. Ives
Concerns of the Church
Preparation for Worship
Meditation .... *Easter Morning* .... de La Tombelle

WORSHIP THE RISEN LORD

Chiming of the Hour
The Call to Worship
Musical Call to Worship .... *Flourish* .... Douglas Wagner
Adult Handbell Choir
Spoken Call to Worship .... Jack Causey

> Christ the Lord is ris'n today,
> Sons of men and angels say,
> Raise your joys and triumphs high,
> Sing, ye heav'ns, and earth, reply.

Hymn of Praise No. 114 .... Easter Hymn
Christ the Lord Is Risen Today
Invocation and Lord's Prayer .... Elmer Piper

WORSHIP THE LOVING CHRIST

Ministry of Hospitality .... Bill Penick
Scripture .... John 15:9-17 .... Ken Lister
Anthem .... *Christ Be in Our Loving* ..... Bob Burroughs
written in honor of Dr. Jack Causey

200

Teacher, preacher, servant, leader, God has given gifts, and grace and faith. Christ be in our loving, our giving and our living. Christ, be in our lifestyle. Make us humble and forgiving. Turn from evil, cling to goodness. Cheerfully give gifts from God and us. Let our living and our loving give to those in need our help, our hope. Christ be in our loving, our giving and our living. Christ be in our lifestyle. Christ be in our lifestyle. Make us humble and forgiving. Christ be in our loving.

The Morning Offering
Hymn of Worship No. 69 .... Azmon
                    O For a Thousand Tongues
Offertory Prayer .... Jack Causey
Offertory .... *An Easter Pastorale* .... L. Boellmann
Doxology

WORSHIP THE GOD WHO GOES AHEAD

Scripture .... Matthew 28:1-7 .... Jack Causey
Invitation to Prayer
Pastoral Prayer .... Bill Penick
Anthem .... *Hallelujah from "Mount of Olives"* .... Beethoven

Hallelujah, unto God's Almighty Son, Praise the Lord, ye bright angelic choirs, in holy songs of joy. Man, proclaim his grace and glory, Hallelujah unto God's Almighty Son. Praise the Lord in songs of joy, O praise the Lord in holy songs of joy. Praise the Lord in holy songs, in holy songs, praise the Lord in songs of joy, in holy songs of joy.

Sermon .... GOD GOES AHEAD OF US ..... Jack Causey
Hymn of Commitment No. 120 .... Darwall
                    Rejoice, the Lord Is King
Benediction
Postlude

The Worship of God

MORNING WORSHIP   November 3, 1985   10:55 A.M.

Broadcast over WMRB—1490 on the Dial

Organ Prelude
Concerns of the Church
Preparation for Worship
Meditation

ALMIGHTY FATHER

Chiming of the Hour
Call to Worship .... Gilbert M. Martin
            When I Survey the Wondrous Cross
Invocation and Lord's Prayer .... Andrew Shull
Hymn of Praise No. 51 .... Redentore
            Great Redeemer, We Adore Thee
Ministry of Hospitality .... Bill Penick

GIVE US A VISION

Scripture .... Luke 22:7-13 .... Jack Causey
The Morning Offering
Hymn of Worship No. 410 .... Lancashire
            We Thank Thee That Thy Mandate
Offertory Prayer .... Ken Lister
Offertory
Doxology
The Lord's Supper

        Scripture .... *1 Corinthians 11:23-26* .... Bill Penick
        Meditation ...... *The Images of Communion* ..... Jack Causey
        The Wafer/Prayer .... Ken Lister
        The Cup/Prayer .... Jack Causey

TO BE YOUR PEOPLE

Scripture . . . . Matthew 5:13-14 . . . . Jack Causey
Anthem . . . . *To Be God's People* . . . . Charles Brown

> Almighty Father, give us a vision of a dying world that needs your love and care. We see the need, the yearning for a Savior, in Jesus' name, grant this our prayer. To be God's people in this place, live His goodness, share His grace, Proclaim God's mercy through His Son, be His love to ev'ryone. And when we falter, be Thou our comfort; Guide us as your children that our lives may be A beacon in this darkness that surrounds us, A light that others then may see. To be God's people in this place, Be His love to ev'ryone.

Meditation . . . . *The Images of Discipleship* . . . . . Jack Causey

IN THIS PLACE

Hymn of Discipleship No. 325 . . . . Footsteps
                        Footsteps of Jesus
Benediction
Choral Benediction . . . . . *Here Is My Life* . . . . Gene Bartlett
Postlude

SUNDAY EVENING WORSHIP

5:00   Youth Choir
      Fellowship Union
6:00   Evening Worship
      Baptismal Service
7:00   Youth Supper
      DiscipleLife

The Worship of God
Sunday, August 24, 1986

MORNING WORSHIP   10:55 A.M.
Broadcast over WMRB—1490 on the Dial

Prelude .... *Largo* .... Handel
Concerns of the Church
Preparation for Worship
Meditation .... *Aria* .... Handel

A MIGHTY FORTRESS IS OUR GOD

Chiming of the Hour
Choral Call to Worship .... G. Young
Come, Christians, Join to Sing
Invocation and Lord's Prayer .... Bill Penick
Hymn of Praise No. 30 .... Lyons
O Worship the King

A BULWARK NEVER FAILING

Ministry of Hospitality .... Bill Penick
Parent/Child Dedication

> Covenant of Dedication
> Minister: "I tell you the truth, unless you change and become like little children, you will never enter the kingdom of heaven. Therefore, whoever humbles himself like this child is the greatest in the kingdom of heaven. And whoever welcomes a little child like this in my name welcomes me." (Matthew 18:3-5)
> Choir: "Train up a child in the way he should go: and when he is old, he will not depart from it." Jesus said, "I am the Way, the Truth, and the Life." (Proverbs 22:6, John 14:6)
> Congregation: "Trust in the Lord with all your heart; and lean not to your own understanding. In all your ways acknowledge Him, and He shall direct your paths." (Proverbs 3:5)

Charge to Parents:
>   Minister: Parents, do you desire that your child grow in the nurture and admonition of the Lord?
>   Parents: **We do.**
>   Minister: As parents, do you covenant with God and with the members of this church to assist your child in growing, as Jesus did, in wisdom and stature and in favor with God and man?
>   Parents: **We do.**
>   Minister: Because you desire for your child a knowledge of the Scriptures and a loving, obedient attitude toward God and His Son, Jesus Christ, do you promise to use your home and the church to accomplish this task?
>   Parents: **We do.**

Charge to Congregation:
>   Minister: Recognizing the responsibility that you have as a congregation toward each child, do you agree to love and protect him, showing always a Christian spirit? Do you promise that by giving your time, talents and money, you will do your part in providing Christian instruction and training? If you will accept this responsibility, say Amen!

Presentation of the Children

Dana Charlotte Boehm (5-3-86) ..... Mr. and Mrs. Dan Boehm
Jon Andrew Guest, Jr. (5-23-86) .... Mr. and Mrs. Jon Guest

Prayer of Dedication .... Raymond Bailey
The Morning Offering
Hymn of Worship No. 37 .... Ein Feste Burg
A Mighty Fortress Is Our God
Offertory Prayer .... Roy Davis
Offertory .... *Andante* .... Mendelssohn
(from Sonata I)
Doxology

HE WILL NEVER FAIL US

Scripture .... Luke 8:22-24 .... Ken Lister
Invitation to Prayer
Pastoral Prayer .... Raymond Bailey

Anthem . . . . *Thy Perfect Love* . . . . John Rutter
Sermon . . . . AN ANSWER TO STRESS . . Raymond Bailey

HIS KINGDOM IS FOREVER

Hymn of Commitment No. 64 . . . . Hyfrydol
Jesus, What a Friend for Sinners
Benediction
Choral Benediction . . . . David Peninger
Depart Now in the Fellowship of God
Postlude . . . . *Allegro* . . . . Handel

---

SUNDAY EVENING SCHEDULE

5:00 p.m.—Youth Choir Begins
5:30 p.m.—Fellowship Training Union
6:00 p.m.—Summer Choir
6:30 p.m.—Evening Worship—Sermon:
"The Power of Positive Thinking"
Dr. Bailey
7:30 p.m.—DiscipleLife

The Worship of God

MORNING WORSHIP Sunday, March 2, 1986 10:55 A.M.

Broadcast over WMRB—1490 on the Dial

Organ Prelude ... *Prelude and Fugue in G-Minor* ...... J. S. Bach
Concerns of the Church
Preparation for Worship
Meditation .... *The Lord's Prayer* .... J. S. Bach

CHRISTIANS, BE COMMITTED

Chiming of the Hour
Call to Worship .... Romans 12:1-2
Choral Call to Worship .... arr. Philip Young
Come, All Christians, Be Committed
Invocation .... Bill Penick
Doxology
Hymn of Praise No. 279 .. *Walk Ye in Him* .... McClard

CHRISTIANS, BE COMMITTED TO SERVE

Ministry of Hospitality .... Elmer Piper
Solo .... *So Send I You* .... John W. Peterson
Ken Lister
The Morning Offering
Hymn of Mission No. 281 .... Message
We've a Story to Tell
Offertory Prayer .... Jack Causey
Offertory .... *Adagio in A-Minor*
Congregational Response to God's Goodness .... *Our Best*

Hear ye the Master's call, "Give Me thy best!"
For, be it great or small, That is His test.
Do then the best you can, Not for reward,
Not for the praise of man, But for the Lord.

Ev'ry work for Jesus will be blest,
But He asks from ev'ryone His best.
Our talents may be few, These may be small,
But unto Him is due Our best, our all.

CHRISTIANS, BE COMMITTED TO SERVE IN LOVE

Scripture .... Galatians 6:13-14 .... Jack Causey
Invitation to Prayer
Pastoral Prayer .... Elmer Piper
Anthem .... *A Call to My People* ...... Bob Burroughs
Sermon .... HOW FAR LOVE REACHES ..... Jack Causey
Hymn of Commitment No. 290 .... Schuler
                    Make Me a Blessing
Benediction
Choral Benediction .. *Christ, Be in Our Loving* ..... Bob Burroughs
Postlude .... *Now Thank We All Our God* .... Karg-Elert

T. MELVIN WILLIAMS, JR.
Decatur, Georgia

[Melvin Williams uses a worship committee to help plan his church's worship services. A brief sketch of his planning process, explanation of the worship committee, and several orders of worship follow.]

Our worship planning process has evolved into a group planning effort by a worship planning team. The planning meeting is open to all members of the church, but we usually have eight or nine people—including the minister of music, organist, minister, and four or five laypeople. Since our church is largely a lay-led congregation, we encourage regular contributions from the members of the congregation.

We meet at 4:45 each Wednesday afternoon to plan two services. We first take a look at the service two weeks ahead. I bring a rough draft of the service. Usually the planning proceeds with the Scripture text and sermon topic for the morning. We then build the service around the theme suggested by the Scripture and sermon. The hymns are carefully chosen by the planners. We also try to make the language inclusive. The choir's music is also selected around the theme for that Sunday. We follow the church liturgical year, so much of our worship life moves through the cycle of Advent, Christmas, Epiphany, Lent, Easter, and Pentecost. We believe our worship belongs in the entire tradition of the church, so we select resources from a variety of Christian traditions. Music spans the gamut from piano improvisations to early American music with dulcimers to Bach and Handel.

[Leslie Withers, a layperson, serves as worship planning coordinator. She describes in further detail the work of the worship committee.]

Overall responsibility rests with the worship and music committee. They do long-range planning and take responsibility for major seasons and holidays, particularly Advent, Lent, and Pentecost.

210

Worship leaders (generally the pastor and minister of music) plan several months ahead the sermon topics, Scripture readings, and special music. Scripture generally is taken from the lectionary.

Detailed planning for Sunday morning services is done by the worship planning group, which meets every Wednesday from 4:45 to 6:00 P.M. Meetings are open to anyone who wants to participate. At least one member of the Worship and Music Committee attends regularly. Leadership is rotated among regular attenders.

We look first at the worship service eleven days away. Someone, generally the pastor, has prepared a rough draft of the service. We suggest changes such as rewording a call to worship to make it easier to read aloud. We particularly look for overall consistency: Do the various parts of the service reflect the theme? Do we have other ideas that would be more appropriate? The rough draft often does not yet have hymns suggested; so we look for those that will fit the mood, theme, and particular function they are to serve (opening hymn of praise, for instance). We also decide who to ask to be liturgist for the service, so that the person can come to worship planning the following Wednesday to become familiar with the service.

Next we look at the worship service four days away. We will have already worked through it the previous week, so this is mainly reconfirming that what we did looks as if it will work. We also decide who should read the Scripture.

Finally, we discuss the previous Sunday's service. What worked well? What didn't fit or didn't go smoothly? What have we learned that we need to remember for future planning?

The Order of Worship

October 5, 1986

WORLD COMMUNION SUNDAY

WE GATHER AS GOD'S PEOPLE

The Concerns and Celebrations of the Congregation
(The Passing of the Friendship Register)
The Organ Prelude .. *Processional for Organ* .... Martin Shaw
The Choir and People (singing alternate lines):

> The Choir: Praise to the Lord, the Almighty, the King of Creation!
> The People: O, my soul, praise him for he is thy health and salvation!
> The Choir: All ye who hear, now to God's temple draw near;
> The People: Join me in glad adoration!
> The Minister: The scripture reminds us "The nations shall march toward your light and their rulers to your sunrise."
> The People: A called people, we are summoned by a promise.
> The Minister: "There are other sheep of mine, not belonging to this fold, whom I must bring in; and they too will listen to my voice. There will then be one flock, one shepherd."
> The People: A people of Christ's purpose, we share his vision.
> The Minister: "From east and west the people will come, from north and south, for the feast in the kingdom of God."
> The People: With thanksgiving we join the varied throng.

*The Hymn of Praise No. 15 .... Lobe Den Herren
Praise to the Lord, the Almighty
(Stanzas 2, 3, & 4)

WE BECOME A PRAYING COMMUNITY

> The Minister: Grace and peace to you from God our creator. Let us celebrate the resurrection of Jesus Christ.
> The People: We gather as his family.
> The Minister: May his love be in our hearts. Let us make our confessions in silence.

*Those who wish may substitute "God" or "God's" for masculine pronouns referring to God.

212

The Silent Prayers of Confession
The Corporate Confession:

> O God, you have created us for life together. Yet we confess that we find it hard to live in peace and justice with one another, within our own community, within our nation, and within the family of nations. We confess that out of fear, uncertainty, and lack of faith we have allowed our nation to stockpile weapons to provide our security, rather than turning to the fulfilling power and promises of your Son, Jesus Christ. Forgive us our small-mindedness. Grant us a fresh sense of your sustaining power, and hold us lovingly as your children, together as the Body of Christ, in whose name we pray.

The Assurance of Pardon
The Moment of Silence
The People Sing .... St. Peter

> In Christ now meet both East and West,
> In Christ meet South and North;
> All Christly souls are one in Him
> Throughout the whole wide earth.

WE HEAR THE WORD

The Old Testament Lesson .... Clay Manley
Amos 5:6-7,10-15
The New Testament Lesson .... Carol Burgess
Luke 17:5-10
The Meditation .... *Amos, the God of Justice* ...... Mel Williams
The Moment of Silence

WE OFFER OUR GIFTS

> The Deacon: What shall I render to the Lord for all bounty given to me?
> The People: I will lift up the cup of salvation and call on the name of the Lord. I will pay my vows in the presence of all God's people.

The Receiving of Gifts
The Offertory .... *St. Peter* .... Arr. H. Max Smith
The People Sing .... St. Peter

> In Christ shall true hearts everywhere their high communion find;
> His service is the golden cord close-binding humankind.

WE CELEBRATE THE HOLY FEAST

The Preparation

> The Minister: The Lord is with you.
> The People: And also with you.
> The Minister: Lift up your hearts.
> The People: We lift them up to the Lord.
> The Minister: Let us give thanks to the Lord our God.
> The People: It is right to give God thanks and praise.

The Litany of Institution *(see insert)*
The Receiving of Bread and Wine
The People Sing . . . . Lasst Uns Erfreuen

> Praise God, from whom all blessings flow;
> Praise God all creatures here below;
> O Praise God, Alleluia!
> Praise God above ye heav'nly hosts,
> Creator, Christ, and Holy Ghost.
> Alleluia! Alleluia! Alleluia! Alleluia! Alleluia!

WE TURN TO THE WORLD

The Prayer for the World (in languages of the world)

> Cynthia Shenk (Dutch)   John Tumblin (Portuguese)
> Matthew Bak (German)   Mike Mears (Russian)
> Dee Ann Coltharp (Japanese)   Pedro Sandin (Spanish)
>   Mike Mears (English)

The Hymn of Faith No. 202 . . . . Duke Street
Jesus Shall Reign Where'er the Sun
(In stanza 4 you may substitute "heirs" for "sons.")
The Benediction
The Choral Postlude . . *O Be Joyful in the Lord* . . . . Martin
(see insert for text)

‡   ‡   ‡

LITURGIST today is Mike Mears.
THE FLOWERS today are given by Frank and Adam King to celebrate the birthday of Robbie King.
NEXT SUNDAY, October 12: Ann Conner is preacher—Hospitality Sunday. We
will also observe Lord's Supper as a sign of Christ's hospitality.

BILL WILLIAMSON
Helena, Arkansas

[Bill is a personal friend and fellow minister in my community. I have long been impressed with his skills in preaching and worship. Bill and I are members of an ecumenical ministerial support group in our town. The group often discusses preaching and worship. I've had the privilege of leading worship with Bill in community services. I've also observed him leading worship in his own church. He has a deep commitment to the priority of worship. Some of Bills' reflections on worship, a few ideas which have worked for him, and his basic order of worship follow.]

"You're lucky, Preacher. You only have to work one day a week." Fortunately, church pastors don't hear a comment like that very often, and when they do, it is usually spoken in jest. Church members recognize that most ministers work a great deal more than one day a week.

Still there is some truth in that comment, truth which ministers would do well to heed. The fact is that the most regular and dependable contact between minister and people takes place in the weekly worship of the congregation. Other kinds of contacts, such as those which take place in times of bereavement or sickness, may be more intensive. But as a colleague of mine once expressed it, "It is in worship that the minister sees most of the people most of the time."

So although the minister's work is not limited to one day a week, much of the work done during the week stands or falls on what happens on that one day of the week when worship takes place. It behooves the minister, then, not to take such times for granted or to go through them in rote fashion. Rather, the time of worship needs to be approached with the care and creativity it well deserves.

Presbyterians do not follow a prescribed liturgy in worship. Yet many congregations follow an order of worship which is similar from week to week. Comfort can be found in following similar routines in worship from one week to the next. Orders of worship which change too radically or which include elements inappropriate to the worship of that congregation cause disorientation and a loss of meaning.

On the other hand, a sameness can lead to dullness, and routine can become mindless rote. The goal in worship is to make changes which are not so radical as to be confusing or offensive but which add vitality and freshness to worship.

In my preparation for worship, I do little changing of the basic order of worship. Most of my efforts are directed at finding fresh ways to invest meaning in old forms. A few examples may suffice.

The Pastoral Prayer.—Often referred to as the "long prayer" (or looong prayer) by many, its posture of bowed heads and closed eyes coupled with the droned platitudes and clichés of the minister, is often more conducive to sleep than to corporate prayer. Sometimes I vary the form somewhat to keep the congregation alert. I have used the bidding prayer, where a subject for prayer is introduced ("Let us pray for those in places of war"), followed by silence, then a brief spoken prayer by the minister. I usually include five or six "biddings" in a single prayer.

The responsive prayer has brief petitions for prayer by the minister, followed by a unison response from the congregation ("We thank you, O God"). This response can be printed in the bulletin or taught to the congregation just before the prayer.

Occasionally, I collect newspaper headlines during the week, then use these as the basis for prayer on Sunday. The headline is read ("Arms Talks Held in Geneva," "Arts Festival Held in City") and then followed by a prayer which is based on that headline.

The Lord's Prayer.—Let's face it: the problem with the Lord's Prayer is that repetition of its familiar words can lead to inattention on the part of those who pray its timeless words. Once I invited a child to come forward and read the prayer while the rest of us listened in silence. Several simple and dignified musical settings of the prayer are available which the congregation can sing.

Unison and Responsive Reading.—Instead of the usual pattern of the minister's reading one line, followed by the congregation's reading the next, I sometimes divide the congregation down the middle and have the two sides alternate the reading. Or, I prepare a reading of a psalm which uses a variety of methods: left side/right side, men/women, soft/loud, etc. Of course, such a reading would have to be printed ahead of time.

This is not an exhaustive list of possibilities, but you get the idea. The point is to discover ways to vary the elements in worship in ways which are appropriate to your congregation. The elements of the service will have a new vitality, and the worship as a whole will have greater meaning to those who participate.

Order of Worship

1st Presbyterian Church, Helena, Arkansas
27th Sunday After Pentecost, November 23, 1986

Rev. W. W. Williamson, Jr., Minister

The Prelude
The Call to Worship (Ps. 95:1-3)

> Leader: O come let us sing unto the Lord
> People: Let us make a joyful noise to the rock of our salvation
> Leader: Let us come into His presence with thanksgiving
> People: Let us worship him with songs of praise
> Leader: For the Lord is a great God
> People: And a great king above all gods.

The Invocation
Hymn 244, Hymnbook .... *Come, Thou Almighty King*
The Prayer for Forgiveness

> God our Father, we confess not only that we have sinned, but we have been accomplices in the sins of others. We have not set examples which would inspire others. Our own wrongdoing has caused some to follow in our way. Our casual discipleship has turned others away from following you. Lord, have mercy upon us. Turn us again to you, not only for our sakes, but for the sakes of those who look to us for guidance. In Christ's name we pray. Amen.

The Assurance of Pardon

Leader: The Lord is merciful and gracious
People: Slow to anger, and abounding in steadfast love.
Leader: Friends, believe the good news of the gospel:
People: In the name of Christ, we are forgiven. Amen.

The Offertory
The Doxology and the Prayer of Dedication
The Anthem
The Pastoral Prayer and the Lord's Prayer
Hymn 510, Hymnbook . . . . *O Beautiful for Spacious Skies*
The Scripture   Colossians 1:11-20
(Pew Bible, p. 184 NT)
The Sermon . . . . UNIVERSAL KING
Hymn 213, Hymnbook . . . . *Crown Him with Many Crowns*
The Confession of Faith . . . . Apostles' Creed
(Page 12—Hymnbook—front of book)
The Gloria Patri
The Benediction and Choral Response
The Postlude

MAYNARD CAMPBELL
Kansas City, Missouri

Maynard Campbell has been involved in worship leadership both from the pulpit and in the classroom. He's served as pastor of several churches and as professor of worship and preaching at Midwestern Baptist Theological Seminary.

Campbell reminds his students that the aim of worship is to encounter the living Lord. When worship leaders become too familiar with the divine, worship is hindered. God is holy. We must never forget that when we lead people to encounter Him in worship.

According to Campbell, primary responsibility for worship belongs to the pastor. While worship responsibilities should be shared, ultimate responsibility is the pastor's. Worship leadership is the pastor's primary calling. It must be his highest priority.

Worship leaders should strive for holistic worship leadership. This includes planning, presiding, and participating. Worship leaders must be intentional in their planning, preside over the worship service with a mood of celebration, and participate with the congregation in the worship of God.

All the elements of worship should be included when we plan worship—praise and adoration, thanksgiving, confession, petition, intercession, proclamation, and commitment. Every element does not have to be included every week, but all must be included on a regular basis.

Campbell suggests having a central theme for every service. This theme will govern the movement of the service. He advocates using interpretative categories as has been illustrated throughout this book. The Bible and hymnbook are the primary resources for finding worship materials. Good worship leaders will attempt to make the worship event relevant to the life of the congregation. Several of Campbell's orders of worship follow.

The Worship of God

April 6, 1975

MORNING WORSHIP

WORSHIP IN PRAISE

Prelude .... Organist

Opening Sentences:

> Minister: Why have you come today?
> People: We have come because the hustle and bustle of daily living has sapped our strength and weakened our spirits.
> Minister: Then, you hope to find renewal for your inner selves here today?
> People: Yes, but we are also here because we are confused and worried about the problems in our world—like the wars in Southeast Asia, the conflicts in the Middle East, the economic insecurity here at home, the increase in crime, the loss of confidence in our nation's leaders.
> Minister: Do you hope to find answers to some of these problems here today?
> People: We know there are no easy answers to complex problems. What we do long for is a Word from the living God that will help us in the living of these days.

Invocation

Hymn of Praise .... *Come Thou Almighty King* 8

Sunday School Report .... Tom Harrison

Welcome to the Worshipers .... Pastor

Announcements .... Pastor

WORSHIP IN STEWARDSHIP

Old Testament Lesson .... Exodus 19:16-19; 20:1-20

Hymn of Devotion ... *How Firm a Foundation* 241

Prayer Requests .... Jesse Moore

Offertory Prayer

Offertory .... Organist

WORSHIP IN WITNESS

Special Music: Medley .... Choir
Hymn of Faith .... *Jesus Is All the World to Me* 142
New Testament Lesson .... Matthew 22:35-40
Special Music .... Dan Givens
Thy Rebuke Hath Broken His Heart/Behold and See
Sermon .... DIGGING THE FOUNDATIONS .... Pastor

WORSHIP IN COMMITMENT

Hymn of Commitment 202
I Need Thee, Precious Jesus
Presentation of New Members .... Pastor
Benediction
Postlude .... Organist

The Worship of God

November 17, 1974

MORNING WORSHIP

THE CELEBRATION OF GOD'S MIGHTY ACTS

Prelude .... Organist

Opening Sentences

> Minister: Let us tell the mighty acts of God
> People: In the beginning God created the heaven and the earth.
> Minister: And God saw everything that he had made, and behold, it was very good.
> People: Thus the heavens and the earth were finished, and all the host of them.
> Minister: But the tragic event of sin has fractured God's creative act. What can God do now?
> People: God says, Behold, I am doing a new thing; now it springs forth, do you not perceive it? For behold, I create new heavens and a new earth; and the former things shall not be remembered or come into mind.
> Minister: This is true, because in the beginning was the Word, and the Word was with God, and the Word was God.
> People: And the Word became flesh and dwelt among us, full of grace and truth.
> Minister: Who is this Word, this Saving Act of God?
> People: He is Jesus, the carpenter of Nazareth. More than this, He is the Christ, the Son of the Living God. (Gen. 1:1,31; 2:1; Isa. 43:19; 65:17; John 1:1, 14; Mark 16:16)

Hymn of Praise .. *Praise to the Lord, the Almighty* 4

Invocation

Sunday School Report .... Tom Harrison

Recognition of Sunday School Workers

Welcome to the Worshipers

THE CELEBRATION OF GOD'S PRESENT ACTION

Hymn of Praise .... *Come Thou Fount* 300
Prayer Requests
Meditation Time
Morning Prayer
Recognition of Our Church's 54th Anniversary

THE CELEBRATION OF GOD'S GOODNESS
THROUGH GIVING

Hymn of Devotion .... *Something for Thee* 366
Offertory Prayer
Offertory .... Organist
Doxology

THE CELEBRATION OF GOD'S WORD
THROUGH PROCLAMATION

Special Music .. *I Sing the Almighty Power of God* .... Choir
Sermon .... A SONG OF CELEBRATION .... Pastor
Hymn of Commitment .... Choir
Is Your All on the Altar?
Presentation of New Members
Benediction
Postlude

EVENING WORSHIP
September 1, 1974

SING TO THE LORD A NEW SONG

Prelude . . . . Organist
Hymn . . . . *Serve the Lord with Gladness* 393
Prayer
Hymn . . . . *There's a Glad New Song* 295
Hymn . . . . *Sweet Peace, the Gift of God's Love* 285
Welcome to the Worshipers

ENTER INTO HIS PRESENCE WITH THANKSGIVING

The Scripture Lesson (from Psalms 105 and 107)

> Minister: O give thanks unto the Lord.
> People: Remember his marvellous works that he hath done.
> Minister: O give thanks unto the Lord,
> People: For He is good: for his mercy endureth forever.

A Time of Thankfulness

> I am Thankful for _____
> I am Thankful for _____
> I am Thankful for _____

Prayer of Thanksgiving . . . . Pastor

HEAR AND OBEY HIS VOICE

Hymn . . . . *Footsteps of Jesus* 333
Offertory Prayer
Offertory
Special Music . . . . Marty Harkey
Sermon . . . . THE LIBERATED CHRISTIAN . . . . Pastor
Hymn of Commitment 203
I Hear Thy Welcome Voice
Benediction
Postlude . . . . Organist

226

APPENDICES

Appendix 1
OUR PLANNING PROCESS
Martin Thielen and Bill Craig

I. BEFORE WE MEET
   A. Long-Range (Quarterly-Annually)
      1. Long-range worship and preaching preparation.
      2. Long-range music preparation.

   B. Weekly
      1. A theme is chosen.
      2. An initial outline is constructed.

II. WHEN WE MEET
   A. We meet every week for worship planning.

   B. We have a time of prayer.

   C. We clarify the theme for Sunday's service.

   D. We construct a final worship outline, based on:
      1. Scripture.
      2. Hymn.
      3. Elements of worship.
      4. Special occasion.

   E. We fill in the outline.
      1. Music.
      2. Scripture.
      3. Prayer.
      4. Proclamation.
      5. Miscellaneous.

III. AFTER WE MEET
   A. Bill: Music Minister
      1. Finalizes music plans.
      2. Prepares final draft of order of worship for secretary.

   B. Martin: Pastor
      1. Writes sermon.
      2. Writes any responsive readings, prayers, etc.
      3. Enlists any laypeople who will be involved.

Appendix 2
TEACHING YOUR CHURCH TO WORSHIP

One of the great needs in our churches today is worship education. Our congregations need to increase their understanding of worship and better experience it. As ministers, we are called to "equip the saints." This is true in the area of worship. While there are many ways to teach people about worship (seminars, workshops, etc,), the best way is through the worship event itself. One of the most effective ways to learn something is to do it. Consider the following ways to teach your congregation about worship during worship services.

You can educate your church about worship through sermons. Numerous Scripture texts are appropriate. Isaiah 6:1-8 has been mentioned several times in this book. It would be an excellent text for preaching on the subject of worship. Genesis 8:13 to 9:1 is another example. This is the story of Noah coming off the ark. His first priority was to worship God. The Psalms offer endless passages for preaching on worship. Consider the following passages for sermon texts on worship: Exodus 3:1-6; Exodus 33:18-23; 2 Samuel 24:18-22; Matthew 2:1-12; Revelation 1 or 5; and a host of others.

Another way to teach your congregation about worship is by interpreting the worship outline at the beginning of the service. Have a place in your order of worship called "Worship Theme Interpretation." Explain the direction of the service. Discuss the various movements of the worship outline for that service. Just a brief time of explanation can teach much about worship.

Brief comments throughout the service can also educate your congregation about worship. Before the Scripture reading for example, explain how this has been an important element of worship since Old Testament days. Before the offering mention that one of the ways we can worship God is through our giving. Have your music minister say a brief word from time to time about music in worship. He could say something about the elements of praise and adoration and then lead in a hymn of praise. Walk your congregation through the worship event, interpreting its meaning along the way. This approach can be effective in educating people about worship.

John Walden, Sr., a pastor in Binghampton, New York, has come up with a great idea for teaching his congregation about worship. It is called

Worship 101: In the Pew Training. He takes the first five minutes of the Sunday morning service to teach about various elements of worshiping God.[1]

This has great potential. You could give brief lessons on what worship is: the priority of worship, theological concepts of worship, etc. You could give brief lessons on the various elements of worship. Explain to your congregation the purpose of the prelude, the call to worship, the invocation, the hymns, the sermon, etc. Explain the various forms of prayer (praise, thanksgiving, confession, intercession and petition, and surrender).

Appendix 3
A FIRST-PERSON SERMON
HE TOOK A TOWEL

A first-person sermon based on John 13:1-15, as told by John, a disciple of Jesus.

(Note: Walk in from the back of the sanctuary. Carry a towel and a wash basin. A costume would make the sermon more effective.)

Good morning. My name is John. I was one of Jesus' disciples. I would like to tell you about some of my experiences with Jesus. You are probably wondering why I brought a towel and a wash basin. Let me explain.

I remember one night in particular, many years ago. It was the time of Passover, and Jesus wanted His disciples to celebrate it together. We met in an upper room in Jerusalem. During the meal Jesus rose from the table, gathered a wash basin like this one, poured out some water, and began to wash our feet. We could hardly believe it. Here was our Master, our Lord, and He was acting like a common servant. It was extremely awkward. Jesus came to Peter. Peter said what we were all thinking. He said, "No Lord, you should not wash my feet!" It seemed so out of place, so wrong. But Jesus insisted that He do so. As we sat in silence while Jesus washed our feet, I began to think about what was happening. Here was our Lord, the Christ, the Son of God, acting like a common slave and washing our feet. And yet, as I thought about it, it was not so strange after all. In a sense, He was always washing the feet of others. He was always a servant, always meeting the needs of people.

The thing that most impressed me about Jesus was His deep compassion and love for people. He cared about people and ministered to their needs.

Jesus cared about people's physical needs. One day we were passing through Jericho. A blind man named Bartimaeus cried out for help. At first I paid him no mind; he was just another blind beggar. But he kept on shouting, "Son of David, have mercy on me!" Jesus heard him shouting. He stopped and walked over to him. Jesus touched his eyes and healed him.

Jesus often helped people who were sick. He healed the blind, the lame, and the mentally ill. I remember when a man with leprosy came to Jesus for help. All the disciples were upset. Nobody wanted to get close to a leper. As we watched, Jesus actually touched this man. We could hardly believe our eyes. Yet Jesus loved him and cared about his suffering. When Jesus touched him, his leprosy went away.

There was a time when five thousand people gathered to hear Jesus teach. The day had come to an end, and everyone was hungry. We advised Jesus to send them away. He said, "Give them something to eat." And with two fish and five loaves of bread, he fed the whole crowd. He often met the physical needs of people.

Jesus also cared about people's emotional needs. He had compassion on those who grieved and those who were depressed, discouraged, or confused. Many times Jesus helped His own disciples when we were emotionally upset. I remember one in particular. It was after Jesus had been killed and resurrected. He was talking to Peter. Peter felt badly about having denied Jesus three times. Jesus said to Peter, "Do you love me?" It hurt Peter because he had failed Him. But Peter did love Jesus and said, "Yes, Lord, I love you." Then Jesus asked him a second time and then a third. Peter was grieved but said for the third time, "Yes, Lord, I love you." After this was over we all realized what Jesus had done. Peter had denied Jesus three times. And now Jesus had given him the opportunity to reaffirm his love three times. Afterwards, Peter and Jesus embraced. I heard Jesus say to Peter, "Peter, I love you, and I forgive you." It was a healing event for Peter. He gained such strength from it. Jesus often met the emotional needs of people.

Jesus also cared about people's spiritual needs. More than anything else, Jesus wanted people to know God. I remember the night Nicodemus came to see Jesus. Jesus told him that he needed to be born again. Jesus was teaching him that people need spiritual life and renewal which only God could provide. Jesus often touched people in such ways. I remember the funny little man named Zacchaeus whose life was changed after his encounter with Jesus.

For three years I followed Jesus. I saw him care about people again and again. He ministered to their needs, whether they were physical, emotional, or spiritual. And he constantly taught us to do the same. He told us that if we wanted to be great we must be servants. He told us over and over, "Care about people; minister to their needs."

I thought of these things that night as Jesus washed our feet. It was a strange night, a scary night. Jesus took bread and wine and said they represented His body and blood, which would be broken and shed for us. He spoke of dying. We didn't understand. After supper we went up on the mountain. Jesus was deeply distressed. He asked Peter, James, and me to pray with Him. He was in great agony. We were so tired, however, that we fell asleep. We woke to the sound of Roman soldiers. It was a nightmare. Jesus was arrested, and we all ran like scared animals.

We kept up with the situation the best we could. We learned that Jesus was being seen by various officials and He was on trial. Then the word came; Jesus was to be crucified. We could not believe it. Why? Because He loved? I felt that my life was caving in all around me. All my hopes and dreams were invested in Jesus, and now they were going to kill Him. He was mocked and beaten and finally led to Golgotha. We were hiding, afraid that we might be next.

Mary, the mother of Jesus, came to me and asked if I would take her to Jesus. I said no at first. I tried to explain that it was a horrible sight to see a man crucified. I was also worried that the officials might recognize us. But Mary persisted, and I finally gave in. As we arrived at the execution site, my stomach was sick. It was a gruesome and horrible scene. Death was everywhere. The people were mocking Jesus, and the Roman soldiers were laughing and having a great time. I was filled with hatred and anger. I was also angry at myself for having failed my Lord. I wanted Jesus to kill them all—the entire, hate-filled crowd. And I knew He had the power to do it, but that He would not.

We moved a little closer to the cross where Jesus hung. He was talking. I could barely make out what He said. It was hard to believe what Jesus was saying. He said, "Father, forgive them." Those animals were killing Jesus, and He was asking God to forgive them!

In spite of His pain and agony, Jesus took time to speak to the man on the cross next to Him. He assured the man that he could be forgiven and would be with God in paradise that very day. He was still meeting the needs of people, all the way to the end. Then Jesus looked directly at me. I felt ashamed. I had run away and deserted Him when the soldiers came. And yet His eyes were filled with love. He also looked at his mother, Mary, who was weeping. Then He said to me, "Behold thy mother!" He then looked at Mary and said, "Behold thy son!" We knew exactly what He was doing. He was making provisions for His mother. He was caring for her needs even as He was dying.

In those last moments all Jesus thought about was others. He was concerned about the people who were killing Him, about the thief next to Him, and about His mother. He was a servant to the end, caring about people and meeting their needs in His death, even as He did in life. He was the man for others, the servant of all. Once again He had a towel in His hands, and He was washing the feet of others.

Of course, you know the story. After the darkness of the cross, God raised Jesus from the dead. And then Jesus established His church to continue His ministry through the ages. Yet I will never forget that night in the upper room when Jesus, the Christ, the Son of God, got down on His hands and knees and washed our feet. And as He did, He taught us a great lesson.

"As I have done to you," He said, "so you should do to others." Jesus was a servant, the man who met the needs of people. Although He was the Christ, He carried a towel in His hands and washed the feet of others. When I think of that night, I recall the words He said so often, "Go and do likewise."

CONCLUSION

Pastoral ministry is a great privilege. I count it a great joy to be involved in leading the church to accomplish its mission to the world, to minister to the needs of people through pastoral care, and to proclaim the gospel to believers and nonbelievers. Part of the ministry of proclamation is to lead worship. I find this to be the most rewarding and enjoyable aspect of ministry. I love to preach and lead worship. I hope you feel the same. It is my prayer that this book will be of value to you as you get ready for Sunday and as you lead your congregation in an encounter with the living Lord through the worship event.

NOTES

Chapter 2: "Filling in the Outline"
1. H. H. Rowley, *Worship in Ancient Israel, Its Forms and Meanings* (Philadelphia: Fortress Press, 1967), pp. 257-71.
2. Donald P. Hustad, *Jubilate! Church Music in the Evangelical Tradition* (Carol Stream, Ill.: Hope Publishing Company, 1961), pp. 92-93. Used by permission.
3. Quoted in Franklin M. Segler, *Christian Worship: Its Theology and Practice* (Nashville: Broadman Press, 1967), p. 36, from Justin Martyr, *The First Apology*, trans. Thomas B. Falls (New York: Christian Heritage, Inc., 1948), p. 107.
4. Quoted in Segler, *Christian Worship*, pp. 45-46, from W. D. Maxwell, *An Outline of Christian Worship* (New York: Oxford University Press, 1955), pp. 56 ff.
5. Quoted in Segler, *Christian Worship*, pp. 49-50, from Earnest A. Payne, *The Fellowship of Believers: Baptist Thought and Practice Yesterday and Today* (London: The Carey Kingsgate Press, Ltd., 1952), p. 92.
6. Quoted in Segler, *Christian Worship*, p. 94, from T. Harwood Pattison, *Public Worship* (Philadelphia: American Baptist Publication Society, 1900), p. 161.
7. Quoted in Segler, *Christian Worship*, p. 95, from Roland Bainton, *Here I Stand* (New York: Abingdon Press, 1950), p. 341.
8. *The Methodist Hymnal: Official Hymnal of the Methodist Church* (Nashville: The Methodist Publishing House, 1961, 1966).

Chapter 3: "Completed Orders of Worship"
1. "Praise the Name of Jesus" by Roy Hicks, Jr. © 1976 Latter Rain Music. All rights reserved. Used by permission of The Sparrow Group.
2. Copyright 1976, Sound III, Inc., 2712 West 104th Terr., Leawood, Kansas. International copyright secured. Used by special permission only.
3. "People Need the Lord" written by Greg Nelson and Phill McHugh. © Copyright 1983 by Shepherd's Fold Music (admin. by Gaither Copyright Mgmnt.) and River Oaks Music Co. (admin. by Tree Publishing Company, Inc.). International Copyright Secured. All Rights Reserved. Used By Permission.
4. G. Temp Sparkman, *Writing Your Own Worship Materials* (Valley Forge, Pa.: Judson Press, 1980), p. 23. Used by permission of Judson Press.
5. Ibid.

Appendix 2: "Teaching Your Church to Worship"
1. John Walden, Sr., *Fresh Ideas for Preaching, Worship, and Evangelism* (Carol Stream, Ill.: Christianity Today, Inc., 1982, 1983, 1984), pp. 46-47.